TOM CUNNINGHAM, BRAD SZOLLOSE & JOHN WESTLEY CLAYTON PRESENT...

POSITIVE MENTAL ATTITUDE

INSPIRING STORIES FROM REAL PEOPLE WHO APPLIED NAPOLEON HILL'S MOST IMPORTANT SUCCESS PRINCIPLE!

TOM CUNNINGHAM, BRAD SZOLLOSE & JOHN WESTLEY CLAYTON PRESENT...

POSITIVE MENTAL ATTITUDE

INSPIRING STORIES FROM REAL PEOPLE WHO APPLIED NAPOLEON HILL'S MOST IMPORTANT SUCCESS PRINCIPLE!

Copyright © 2017 by John Westley Publishing

Publishers: John Westley Clayton

www.johnwestley.com

info@johnwestley.com

& Tom Cunningham

www.tom2tall.com

tom@tom2tall.com

ISBN 978-0-9976801-9-5

All Rights Reserved.

No part of this publication may be reproduced, distributed, or transmitted in any form or by any means, including photocopying, recording, or other electronic or mechanical methods, or by any information storage and retrieval system without the prior written permission of the publisher and/or individual contributing author, except in the case of very brief quotations embodied in critical reviews and certain other noncommercial uses permitted by copyright law.

Cover Photo Credit:

Happy young businessman and big city

ShutterStock ID: 93945211

By Iakov Kalinin

Table of Contents

Dedication — i
Acknowledgements — ii
Foreword — vi
Testimonials — x
Introduction — xvi

CHAPTER 1 — 1
The Science Behind
Positive Mental Attitude
By: Dr Tamara Tilleman

CHAPTER 2 — 17
My Journey Through a Dream
By: Brianna M. Lyons, MPH

CHAPTER 3 — 27
The Business of Life
By: Matthew Vincent Gold

CHAPTER 4 — 33
How I Built An 8-Figure Company With
No Experience (And So Can You)
By: Jeffery Feldberg

CHAPTER 5 — 59
I Don't Paint Rust Anymore
By: Scott Venezia

CHAPTER 6 — 73
Surviving Death Valley Helped
Us Find Our Way
By: Rachael Dilling

CHAPTER 7 — 83
The Fine Art of Parenting After Separation
The Power of a Positive Mental Attitude
By: Cynthia (Bester) Vos

CHAPTER 8 — 97
GRATITUDE FOR VICTORIOUS LIVING
By: Christy Onabu

CHAPTER 9 — 109
Staying Positive In a Hectic Negative World
By: Peter Kamerman

CHAPTER 10 — 121
If You Change Your Thinking
You Change Your Reality
By: Alex Alfaro

CHAPTER 11 — 133
Your Success Puzzle
By: Gary Burleson

CHAPTER 12 — 145
Positive Mental Attitude
By: Ann McNeill

CHAPTER 13 — 155
To Whom Much is Given
Much Is Required
By: Linda (Nefertiti) Patton

CHAPTER 14 — 173
Samson vs Goliath:
Using PMA To Grow A
Startup Against Cable Giants
By: Mark English

CHAPTER 15

What Will You Do To Change?
By: Antony Scandale

Napoleon Hill Bio	194
The Seventeen Principles	196
About Tom "too tall" Cunningham	197
About Brad Szollose	198

Dedication

This book is first dedicated to the millions, even tens of millions, of **ROCK STARS** across this beautiful earth that work daily to display a Positive Mental Attitude to their fellow human to make our world a better place.

Second, and *most importantly*, this book is dedicated to the rest of the people of the world who struggle with displaying a Positive Mental Attitude.

May you use the stories within this book to create a Positive Mental Attitude within your soul, on your way to gaining possession of your own mind.

There's a whole new world that awaits you on the other side of negativity.

"You are who and what
you create yourself to be"
— John Westley Clayton

Acknowledgements

Dear Reader,

Congratulations!

Congratulations on what, you ask?

The mere fact that you're reading this book tells me you're serious about your success.

Success.

Seven letters that means so much.

Whether you're just starting out for the first time, or instead, you're already successful and want to scale, this book is for you.

If you've tried and failed before in the past, I have great news for you.

It's not your fault.

There so much misinformation that most people are doomed to fail before they start.

And that's where this book comes in.

You see, my dear reader, success leaves clues.

This book is filled with success stories from people who are just like you.

People just like me, you ask?

Impossible, you say!

You may be thinking that you're not smart enough. Perhaps you believe that you don't have enough money. You might even believe that you don't have enough education or experience. Maybe you wonder if you have what it takes to even be successful.

If you're thinking any of those thoughts, stop right now.

Stop now, and instead, let's look at me.

I was a kid right out of school who had no money, experience, or team. All I had was an idea.

On paper, I should have failed before I even started.

Yet, despite this, I built a highly profitable 8-figure company that helped change the social fabric of society.

Some people, perhaps even you, may say that I was lucky. You could even say that I was at the right place at the right time.

All I know is the harder I worked the luckier I became.

What's my secret, you ask?

I stumbled on success principles that are as old as success itself.

And the man who introduced me to these timeless success principles is the Success Whisperer himself, Napoleon Hill.

Napoleon Hill and his principles on a Positive Mental Attitude (PMA) have stood the test of time. Hill has shown time and time again that there is a precise methodology for success. Hill dedicated his life to finding and documenting these seemingly elusive principles through fascinating stories in his books.

With over 100 million copies sold, Napoleon Hill's book, Think and Grow Rich, has helped create more successful people than any other book, ever.

A book on its own is just a book. A heartfelt thanks to Don Green and the Napoleon Hill Foundation team who tirelessly ensure new generations of entrepreneurs have the privilege and benefit of experiencing Hill's success formula.

If not for the passion, care, and commitment of Tom "*too tall*" Cunningham this book would not exist. Tom is a living and breathing embodiment of a Positive Mental Attitude. The mere fact that Tom figured out how to work with 16 entrepreneurs and collect their stories speaks to Tom's PMA! Despite the challenges, Tom's persistence, patience and kindness made all the difference.

If a picture is worth a thousand words, there are not enough words to thank Brad Szollose whose vision, passion, and talent shine through in creating the cover of this book.

A big thank you for John Westley Clayton. John Westley is our talented, passionate, and dedicated publisher who ensures everything is just right. An idea remains an idea unless the idea is properly executed. John Westley, thank you for thinking through every aspect of this book before bringing it to market.

And last, but certainly not least, are the 16 individuals whose stories fill these pages. Within these pages is a treasure trove of success principles for you to use and make your own.

Every single person comes into this world with a special gift. Find your gift, and figure out how to help through your gift and success is yours. You'll write your own ticket.

Listed in alphabetical order are my esteemed authors who took their most valuable resource, their time, and dedicated it to share their stories for your sole benefit. Thank you:

Alex Alfaro, Cyndi Bester, Gary Burleson, Rachael Dilling, Mark English, Jeffrey Feldberg, Matthew Vincent Gold, Brianna Lyons Harris, Peter Kamerman, Ann McNeill, Christy Onabu, Linda (Nefertiti) Patton, Antony Scandale, Dr. Tamara Tilleman, Scott Venezia, and Khuram YasinMy

The next time you face a difficult challenge remember the wise words of Napoleon Hill who wisely said that:

> *"There is very little difference in people, but that little difference makes a big difference. The little difference is attitude. The big difference is whether it is positive or negative."*

And if you're wondering when you can start achieving, once again, Napoleon Hill said it best with,

> *"Your big opportunity may be right where you are now."*

Here's to you and your success!

Your Raving Fan,

Jeffrey E. Feldberg

8-Figure Entrepreneur

www.jeffreyfeldberg.com

Foreword

As you can imagine, maintaining a Positive Mental Attitude (PMA) while serving 42 years as a police officer, including working in the homicide division, was extremely challenging. Dealing with criminals and crimes, including homicides, could have easily caused me to take on a negative attitude and to assume the worst of people. Thankfully, I worked with some great people in my police career and came across enough good people that my PMA remained intact on the job most of the time.

Although I did not read *Think and Grow Rich* by Napoleon Hill until I was 68 years old, at the insistence of Greg Reid, author of *Three Feet From Gold*, I used Hill's Success Principles, especially PMA, during my career as a police officer and to help create and co-found The Make-A-Wish Foundation.

I learned from Greg Reid, and *Think and Grow Rich*, that Definiteness of Purpose was considered the most important of the 17 Principles of Success in Napoleon Hill's opinion. Hill's business partner, W. Clement Stone, co-author with Hill of the book *Success Through A Positive Mental Attitude*, argued that PMA was the most important success principle.

I had a Positive Mental Attitude long before I knew my Definite Purpose, and it served me well in everything I did, and so I believe that PMA has been the key to my overall success in life.

Like many people, I did not discover my Purpose until later in my life, when I was 37 years old. For those of you not familiar with how The Make-A-Wish Foundation got started, let me share the story with you.

It all started when U.S Customs Agent Tommy Austin and Arizona Department of Public Safety Detective Ron Cox were working together on a drug stakeout and Austin told Cox about a 7-year old boy named Chris, who had terminal leukemia and wanted to be a Highway Patrol Motorcycle Officer like his heroes Ponch and Jon from the then popular television series "CHiPS". Running into bureaucratic hesitation at Customs, Austin asks Cox if the Arizona Department of Public Safety can possibly do something.

Cox takes the request to DPS spokesman Allan Schmidt, who asks DPS Director Ralph Milstead. He gives Schmidt carte blanche to grant Chris' wish.

Soon Austin received a call from Chris' mom saying that she doesn't think he can hang on much longer.

"None of us had any idea what we were getting into at the time," Schmidt will recall years later. He draws other people in: Officer Jim Eaves will bring his patrol car, and Officer Frank Shankwitz his motorcycle, to meet the DPS helicopter flying Chris to headquarters. On April 29, Chris comes from Scottsdale Memorial Hospital to the empty lot by DPS at Lewis and 19th Avenue. There he meets Highway Patrol Motorcycle Officer Frank Shankwitz for the first time and right ways asks if he can get on his motorcycle. Following that meeting, Chris and his parents are giving a tour of the Highway Patrol headquarters and that's when Lt. Col. Dick Schaefer gave the boy a "Smokey Bear" hat and one of his own old badges, and Chris becomes Arizona's first and only honorary Arizona Highway Patrol officer.

Everyone who meets the beaming boy chewing bubble gum wants to help. At the end of the day, some of those involved meet in a spontaneous group hug and realize they don't want the day to be the end of it. They also know they don't have much time.

Two of them, Cox and Eaves, go to John's Uniforms, the business that makes all Highway Patrol uniforms, and order one in Chris' size. Two ladies work all night to have it ready the next day. Led by Shankwitz and several other motor and car officers they take the uniform to his house. After Chris receives his uniform, Shankwitz sets up cones for Chris to steer his battery-powered motorcycle through to qualify for a motorcycle officer's wings. Of course Chris passes his test and asks Shankwitz, *"When do I get my motorcycle wings"*?

Shankwitz orders the custom-made motorcycle wings and picks them up a couple of days later. As he is leaving the jewelers, he is notified that Chris is back in the hospital, in a coma and will probably not survive the day. Shankwitz goes to the hospital and Chris' uniform is hanging right by his bed. Just as Shankwitz pins on the motorcycle wings, Chris awakens from the coma, sees his motorcycle wings on his uniform and has a big smile and says thank you. He passed away later that day. Shankwitz also hoped those wings helped carry him to heaven

When Chris died, commanders from the Highway Patrol said we had lost a fellow officer and asked Officers Frank Shankwitz and Scott Stahl to fly back to Illinois for his funeral. Chris was buried in uniform and given the ceremony of a fellow fallen officer.

From the time the two officers land in Chicago to when they leave again, word spreads of their story, and they are amazed at how strangers are affected by it. Flying home to Arizona from Chris' funeral, Shankwitz starts thinking how they had made Chris' *"Wish"* come true, and why couldn't he do that for other children with life-threatening illness, let them *"Make-A-Wish"* and make it happen

A few weeks after returning to Arizona, Shankwitz attends a District Highway Patrol BBQ and tells several attending about his idea to start a non-profit that grants wishes to children with life-threatening medical conditions. The majority told him it would never work, but a few did listen and agreed to help and become board members. The birth of the foundation was on it's way.

The first donation is $15, given to Shankwitz by a grocery store manager. For month records, bills and change are kept in envelopes carried around by founders. In November of 1980 the group receives its tax-exempt status as a non-profit organization and Shankwitz is voted in as the first President/CEO. In March 1981, the group has raised $2000 and can grant its first official "*wish.*"

Since that first wish, not only have I discovered my Definite Purpose, I have met and communicated with many, many great people who are helping to make this world a better place. Their work and effort is creating lasting memories for parents and kids that will never be forgotten. It is much easier to maintain a Positive Mental Attitude, surrounded by such amazing people, compared to my career as a police officer.

Life is like that in some ways. You have to purposefully choose to think, speak, and act positively while doing things that are not enjoyable and often very negative.

Even once you have discovered your Definite Purpose you will still have to do things you do not enjoy doing however, knowing your Purpose and maintaining your PMA, becomes much easier.

The stories in this book will encourage you to purposefully and deliberately choose a Positive Mental Attitude in all areas of your life. The authors have opened their lives to you, sharing the good and bad, so that you understand how tough it is to be positive, and what the rewards of doing it will do for you.

We all need stories like these so we can think about them, and their lessons, when negative thoughts start drifting through our mind. It requires a lot of effort to manage and direct your 60,000 to 70,000 daily thoughts. However, it is well worth it, both for yourself and everyone you encounter when you make that choice.

Frank Shankwitz

Creator and Co-Founder of Make A Wish Foundation

For more info: http://www.wishman1.com/

Testimonials

"Rare do you find a resource packed full of wisdom of the ages and focused on helping you understand the power of your mind, the importance of your attitude, and the reality that you are more capable than you thought possible to achieve your goals and live your dreams! Positive Mental Attitude will super-charge your passions and desires, and breathe air under your wings to help you soar towards your own Journey to Success!"

Chuck Bolena, M.Ed.
President, Results From Thinking
ResultsFromThinking.com

"What is the purpose of Life if not to be happy? Above all other desires, goals and dreams, if we are not happy, we are not truly living. I would argue that happiness is the ultimate pursuit and achievement for humanity and so it must start with a PMA. My study and practice over the last 8 years of living purposefully with a PMA every single day has changed me and I believe that that every person has the same chance and choice to become more aware of their level of positivity and to increase it for a better life. This book will be an amazing companion for anyone looking to be happier because as we read these stories and shining examples of PMA in action, we get to decide how we can also become examples to those around us and help spread positivity to world. Thank you to the authors for sharing their stories and staying positive!"

Dave Doyle
PMA Professor, TEDx Speaker, Author, Napoleon Hill Trainer
https://www.facebook.com/pmadave/
pmaprofessor@gmail.com

"This book is not just words on a page but living proof that your choices determine your path in life. Each one of these incredible author's journey starts with their choice to be positive in their thinking. With their Positive Mental Attitude they have discovered their Definiteness of Purpose as the foundation for their life. The focus on the purpose and following the Success Principles that were written about in 1937 showing how pertinent they are today. Following them with the right attitude, PMA you will overcome the bumps in your journey to success. As I read this book it was reinforced in me to stay positive and focus on my definiteness of purpose. Learn from these authors and follow your purpose and CHOOSE to have a POSITIVE MENTAL ATTITUDE, live the Success Principles of Napoleon Hill and we will see you in the land of success."

David L. Brown
Business Plan Answer Man
International Bestselling Author
www.businessplananswerman.com

"I have learned that I can gain tremendous value from reading the experiences of other people's challenges, struggles, and successes, and apply these learnings to my life, helping me progress towards my goals and desires.

"This book is a must read to help you solidify the fundamental principle of having a Positive Mental Attitude in any stage of your journey. Read, take notes, and learn from these successful authors and apply the same principles to your game plan and watch what happens!"

Dr. Ron Jenkins
Executive Consultant, Ambit Energy

"Too many people underestimate the important role that mindset plays in empowering one to create the lifestyle they deserve. This book is a wonderful resource that helps the reader not only understand mindset but take positive actions to adopt one that allows them to evolve."

Glenn Garnes
Founder
Village Connector Community
http://VillageConnector.com

"I am massively impressed! The story telling ability of these writers has you yearning for the next page and each of their life experiences are lessons for everyone on earth! What you get out of this book is a high on life I can do it too attitude that brightens your day, spirits, relationships and success!

Diana Dentinger
Creator of the Personality & Needs Profile™
https:// www.dianadentinger.com

"Without a Positive Mental Attitude, I would be one of the many unfortunate people buried in mass graves in Cambodia, when millions of Cambodians were executed by the Communist Khmer Rouge.

PMA helped me during my escape and journey to freedom in the United States and it will help you get the most out of every area of your life.

Every story in this book will direct or redirect your life towards your Purpose. Read it with a PMA and apply it to achieve your goals and create a legacy of your life."

Timothy Chhim
International Bestselling Author
Napoleon Hill Foundation Certified Instructor
Napoleon Hill Foundation licensee for the country of Cambodia
Inspirational Speaker

"Like a big tree that needs water to keep growing tall, Positive Mental Attitude (PMA) is the magic nutrient that keeps it moving up and providing shade to all those who take refuge under it. There isn't a day that goes by where I don't call on PMA to help me in some way, even if its to help remember the beautiful things that surround me right now.

This is the one book in Tom Cunningham's arsenal of books that can make a significant change in your life as you read it. Absorbing these wonderful stories will put you *"in spirit"* and help you connect to others with a greater inner resolve."

Be blessed and remember…PMA all the way!

Taylor Tagg
Author / Spiritual Advisor / Speaker
ForgiveandFindPeace.com

"If you are looking for inspiration, guidance, or hope these authors prove there is always a way to achieve your goals and it starts with the power of positive thinking!! The biggest and hardest step to breaking through to the next level is all in your head. This book is a definite must read!"

Sarah Steinerstauch
Operations Manager
Biologica Environmental Services
www.biological.ca

"The power of positive thinking has been something that I have intuitively known to be a path to success, but it is very gratifying to see stories shared in print from people who have mastered this state of mind and are willing to share their stories. Keeping the past in the past and not allowing it to drag down your plan for the future, and forgiveness of anybody to whom you have assigned blame were two of the techniques that I think I will personally return to over and over."

Sara Stamm
Registered Massage Therapist
http://www.ascendamassage.ca/

"Positive Mental Attitude is a wonderful addition to your personal library for success! I have used many of these same principles but still learned very important methods from this book that can be applied in my everyday life. It is true that when great minds come together great things happen. The stories and experiences in this book come from highly successful people that are touching and relatable. It is a must read if you are wanting to win more in life."

Adrian Starks
Motivational Speaker
www.championup.net

"Inspiring stories of loss, learning, failure, success, bravery and choices. I was able to relate to some of the experiences of the various writers contributions. I liked the inherent theme of positivity and choice. Take the time to read this book and discover that you have the ability and power to have a happy, healthy, successful life."

Amanda Carl
Administrative Assistant
Investors Group
www.investorsgroup.com

Introduction

First published in 1937 during the Great Depression, at the time of Napoleon Hill's death in 1970, *Think and Grow Rich* had sold more than 20 million copies, and by 2015, over 100 million copies had been sold worldwide, according to Wikipedia.

Wow! That's a lot of books and *Think and Grow Rich* continues to be a sales sensation today, 80 years after it was first published; this is a must have, must read book!

Why would I address a timeless classic during an introduction to a *Journey to Success* series on Positive Mental Attitude? Because the author, Napoleon Hill, developed the importance of this principle through *Think and Grow Rich*, and he joined forces with W. Clement Stone and wrote *Success Through a Positive Mental Attitude*, another classic that you must have, read, and study. These two pioneers show you how vital it is to have a positive mental attitude as a way of life to achieve great success and the stories you are about to read support this philosophy and demonstrate its importance time and again.

Hill writes, *"As you read this philosophy for the first time, then, when you reread and study it, you will discover that something has happened to clarify it, and give you a broader understanding of the whole. Above all, do not stop, nor hesitate in your study of these principles until you have read the book at least three times, for then, you will not want to stop."* This is strong advice directly from Mr. Hill himself, *"At least three times, for then, you will not want to stop."* I think he was instructing you and me to read this book [*Think and Grow Rich*] more than three times. How do you interpret this?

More advice from Mr. Hill: *"If you choose to follow some of the instructions but neglect or refuse to follow others – you will fail! To get satisfactory results, you must follow all instructions in a spirit of faith.*" This is crystal clear, right? "*You must follow all instructions.*" You need to understand, Think and Grow Rich is literally an instruction manual for success.

Do you want to be successful? Yes? Then here's what you need to do: Read *Think and Grow Rich* like a scientist, following each instruction to the T, step by step. Also, you need to read each story in this book with the mindset that 'successful people always leave clues.' As you figure out what these clues are, you are on your way, because each author in this book is incredibly successful and freely sharing his or her secrets for success with you! Once you discover their clues, all you need to do then is copy, copy, copy, and take action at once to implement these principles in your life.

As you will discover, having a positive mental attitude alone is not sufficient to achieve success. You need to internalize and master other key principles in order to catapult your efforts forward. Please allow me the opportunity to share with you some of the clues upfront. These principles have served me very well. As you read each story, observe how the authors applied one or more of the following in their journey:

1. **Willpower.** This is having self-mastery, self-discipline, and self-control. This is a driving element pushing you closer to your goals. Another critical component is knowing your 'why' – the reason you do what you do and want what you want. Your 'why' pulls you and your willpower drives you further than you ever thought possible.
2. **Persistence.** This is being ceaseless towards your goals, and having the tenacity not to give up. Martin Luther King, Jr. once said, "*If you can't fly then run, if you can't run then walk, if you can't walk then crawl, but whatever you do you have to keep moving forward.*"
3. **Time.** Consider your actions on a day-by-day basis, then week-by-week, and month-by-month, and year-by-year. This is a lifelong commitment, and

you need to stay the course and weather the storms. The American Actor, Adrien Brody, said, *"my dad told me, 'It takes fifteen years to be an overnight success,' and it took me seventeen and a half years."*

4. **Repetition.** Over and over and over again. You must maintain constant vigilance to succeed. Earl Nightingale said it best, "Whatever we plant in our subconscious mind and nourish with repetition and emotion will one day become a reality." Napoleon Hill wrote, *"Repetition of affirmation of orders to your subconscious mind is the only known method of voluntary development of the emotion of faith."*

5. **Hard work.** This is not easy; know this from the start. This may be difficult depending on where you are in your journey towards having a Positive Mental Attitude and use of the principles found in this book. These authors are regular people just like you and I. If they can do it, you can do it too; you must have faith!

6. **Setbacks.** I bet you're surprised to see this in a list of success principles. You must know ahead of time; there will be setbacks. When they come, relax! This is the key to getting back on track quickly and stay on track longer. Lindsey Vonn, an American World Cup Alpine Ski Racer on the US Ski Team, stated, *"setbacks motivate me."* Let them motivate you.

7. **Patience.** This is required and, please, be kind to yourself. Are you progressing towards your goal? Think progression, not perfection. Be kind to yourself when you have setbacks, focus on the good things you are doing and commit to a better day tomorrow. Every single day is an opportunity for you to start anew; I call this my '24-hour Reset Button.' Each new day stands alone and brings you another chance to move closer towards your goals, so make each day a Great Day! Napoleon Hill

wrote, "*Patience, persistence, and perspiration make an unbeatable combination for success.*"

8. **Desire.** I call this Yougottawanna! You must want to do this; I mean really want to! You must develop a burning desire to achieve your goal. Know you can! Plato wrote, "*Human behavior flows from three main sources: desire, emotion, and knowledge.*" Yougottawanna!

9. **Faith.** This I call Yesican! You must believe you can. If anyone else can do this, you can do this as well. Yes, you can! Helen Keller said, "*Optimism is the faith that leads to achievement. Nothing can be done without hope and confidence.*" Remember, "*desire (Yougottawanna) backed by faith (Yesican) knows no such word as impossible.*" —Napoleon Hill.

Here's my challenge for you. Get a notebook and write the following principles down–willpower, persistence, time, repetition, hard work, setbacks, patience, desire, and faith. As you read this particular series of chapters take notes as you discover these and other critical principles presented in the stories that follow. Remember, successful people always leave clues. Learn to look for and copy the clues that will help you become more successful too, in all areas of life – health, wealth, love, happiness, and spirit! After reading this book, pick up *Think and Grow Rich* and read it one more time (or maybe for the first time). You will be glad you did.

I leave you with my daily prayer that I learned from Napoleon Hill. I repeat this prayer, aloud, in front of the mirror six times in the morning and six times in the evening – every single day!

I ask not for more riches, but more wisdom with which to accept and use wisely the riches I received at birth in the form of the power to control and direct my mind to whatever ends I desire. Thank You! Thank You! Thank You!

This one prayer is the secret to my success going forward. Health, wealth, love, happiness, and spirit – all five! I love this prayer. This prayer embodies the clue discovered by Napoleon Hill when he was being coached by Andrew Carnegie. Carnegie told him of a great power which is under his control. *"The power to take possession of your own mind and direct it towards what ever ends you desire."* I am taking possession of my own mind, and directing it towards ends of my own choice. Are you?

The riches discovered in this book can change your life forever! Take your time to read each chapter, highlight key points, take notes, think like a scientist and discover the clues left behind for you to pick up. Most of all enjoy the stories freely shared by some incredible people from across the globe who suffered failures and ultimately climbed their way to success. Be inspired and know you can do the same.

I'll leave you with one of my favorite quotes by Henry Ford:

*"Whether you think you can, or you think you can't – **you are right!**"*

Thank you,

Jim Shorkey

JimShorkey1957@gmail.com

www.ResultsfromThinking.com

CHAPTER 1

The Science Behind Positive Mental Attitude

By: Dr Tamara Tilleman

"Nothing can stop the man with the right mental attitude from achieving his goal; nothing on earth can help the man with the wrong attitude"

— Thomas Jefferson, Founding Father, principal author of the Declaration of Independence and the 3rd President of US. (1743-1826)

Introduction

Napoleon Hill in his iconic work gave 17 principles to unlock one's personal achievements. He detailed how to prime one's mind to a more positive optimistic state and how using positive mental attitude (PMA) can clear obstacles on one's way to a successful life. It takes a positive attitude to achieve positive results. Therefore a positive and optimistic mental attitude is appropriate even under adverse circumstances. This important foundational element of success emphasizes that you, and only you, are the most important factor in creating your own success. Your mindset and the awareness of it will enable new and better ways of handling situations and will reward you throughout your life.

Although Napoleon Hill made these observations years ago, modern research supports the important role that attitude plays in determining one's quality of life, success, physical and mental health and even longevity. In this review, we will examine the evidence for favorable outcomes linked to positive attitude. In addition, since simply finding an association between positive attitude and benefits such as good health does not prove that good attitude is contributing to good health, we will look for evidence of a causal relationship. We will look at studies showing that one can influence outcomes by inducing (priming, preconditioning or anchoring) a positive mental attitude. We will also consider potential physiologic mechanisms through which attitude may exert effects on outcomes.

So let's start by asking some basic questions.

1st Question:
What exactly are positive thoughts, feelings, and attitudes?

Positive Thinking/Thoughts is the first step to setting your mind to focus on the bright side of life. An example of a positive/happy thought can be: "*I would like to have a cold ice cream on this sunny summer day*". Any thought in our mind can either be ignored or be interpreted and converted into a feeling. Thoughts that are not backed up with the emotions will disappear.

Positive Emotions is the second step in the action chain when a thought is converted into a feeling, experience, or emotion. Emotions are physical manifestations of our thoughts, and they are the energy behind any success. Emotions start the excitement even before the event has happened. Going on with the ice cream example, I can either ignore the ice cream thought or I can start feeling joyful for a sweet cool treat. I may start fantasizing about the taste of my favorite flavor -- lemon tart-- and even salivate. Emotions may do the opposite if I am on a diet and the thought of an ice cream stresses me out, making me sad or angry.

When thoughts are converted into emotions, we start building up an energy that will ignite movement/motion (e-motion) and will enable us to progress. This is when we become creative or become resilient, capable of handling obstacles during any journey.

Positive Attitude/Positive Mental Attitude/or Positive Optimistic Attitude is the third step.

Attitude is formed when one's thoughts and emotions lead to a more generalized outlook, stance or opinion. It is commonly expressed as a position of the body indicating an action or mental state.

Attitude often is manifested in **behavior,** the collection of habitual actions that reflect the individual's state of mind. A positive mental attitude can enhance passion and perseverance for your goals, especially for long-term goals.

2nd Question:
What evidence do we have that attitude influences outcome?

There is a growing body of literature on explanatory style (e.g., optimism-pessimism) and how it influences our survival. Those who have a pessimistic explanatory style are more prone to depression, have poorer health, exhibit reduced immune function, experience faster decline of cognitive functions and have a shorter survival rate compared to optimists. By using scales such as the Optimism-Pessimism Scale (PSM), in 2006 Brummett assessed attitude of students who entered the University of North Carolina. During a 40-year follow-up of 6,958 of these students, 476 deaths occurred. What was of interest in this study was that mental attitude of pessimism versus optimism measured years earlier influenced longevity. Really pessimistic individuals (those who scored in the upper tertile) had decreased rates of longevity compared with optimistic individuals who scored in the bottom tertile of the distribution (Brummett, 2006). In another cohort study, optimistic Danish individuals enjoyed increased longevity whereas pessimistic individuals in both women and men incurred higher death rates compared to neutral individuals (Engberg, 2013). Even cancer patient survival can be influenced by mental attitude. A study from the Mayo Clinic College of Medicine reviewed 534 lung cancer patients. All had had their attitude evaluated by the Minnesota Multiphasic Personality Inventory scale performed 20 years prior to their sickness. Among those lung cancer patients, the ones having a pessimistic explanatory style experienced a less favorable survival outcome (Novotny P, 2010).

To conclude: Optimism is linked to increased longevity and better health outcomes.

3rd Question:
What does science say about our ability to influence our brain? Can we alter results by preconditioning our mind?

In 2002 Princeton Professor Daniel Kahneman was awarded the Nobel Memorial Prize in Economic Sciences for applying psychological insights into human behavior to explain economic decision-making (Nobel Prize, 2002). This was a remarkable achievement for a psychologist who had never taken a course in economics. Kahneman and his colleague Amos Tversky explored for decades the anchoring phenomenon (focalism), a cognitive bias that describes the common human tendency to heavily rely on the first piece of information offered (the "anchor") when making decisions. The researchers showed how such preconditioning of the brain can influence judgment and decision-making.

The Science Behind Positive Mental Attitude

In one study they asked people to guess the percentage of African countries represented in the United Nations. However, the guess took place several minutes after those people spun a number wheel (Tversky Amos, 1974). The researchers showed that the first piece of information (number generated by spin of the wheel) had a marked effect on the UN estimates (decision making). People who first spun a high number guessed higher estimation than people who spun a lower number on the wheel. Even payoffs for accuracy did not reduce the anchoring effect.

Several years later Helen Langer, a Psychology Professor from Harvard University, began studying the psychology of unconscious behavior and decision-making processes. She was the first one to show that the mind is so powerful that even medical symptoms (such as aging symptoms) can be reversed if well anchored. Langer had worked with residents of nursing homes in Massachusetts. Her work with Dr. Rodin published in 1976 suggests the mind can influence the body so that negative consequences of aging may be prevented or reversed. Even small anchoring as watering a plant can result in a significant 50% lower death rate in that nursing home (Langer E. J., 1976).

Though science needs to be skeptical of any evidence from such small underpowered studies (that were not designed to research mortality) (Coyne J., 2014) (Andrew, 2015), this study generated widespread interest and controversy. Among the most notable reactions was a Time magazine article heading: *"What is age if nothing but a mindset?"* (Grienson, 2014). Building upon her work at the nursery home, Langer designed a study showing that even a short-term intervention/anchoring can influence the mind-body connection and result in better health. In that groundbreaking research, Dr. Langer took 2 groups of men in their 70s and 80s for a week of retreat in a New Hampshire monastery. The entire monastery was converted into a scene from some 20 years earlier, with Perry Como songs from a vintage radio, Ed Sullivan playing on a black and white TV, authentic old magazines, movies, music, books and other things all from 1959, the year the Barbie Doll was launched. What an interesting year it was, 1959. Alaska becomes the 49th State and Hawaii becomes the 50th state, Fidel Castro comes to power in Cuba, the Soviet Union crashes the Luna 2 spacecraft into the Moon, the Dalai Lama and tens of thousands of Tibetans flee to India and the Los Angeles Dodgers win the World Series (1959 events). On the big screen, the epic film "*Ben-Hur*" is released along with my favorite comedy "*Some Like it Hot*". Charlton Heston and Jack Lemon will both win an Oscar for their roles, but that would happened a year later in 1960.

Dr. Langer created 2 study groups with similar ages, diseases, and numbers of participants. The only difference in the study was that for a whole week the first group was instructed to talk about what happened 20 years earlier and the other group was instructed to live and act as if they were living in 1959. The entire experiment consisted of a talk versus acting as if you are living 20 years earlier. The outcomes were shocking; the aging symptoms of the acting group started to reverse, with changes in their arthritis, their gait, their handgrip, their flexibility, their hearing and even their height (Langer E. J., 2009). Associating with a younger version of themselves, these group members had the power to reverse some of the aging symptoms within a week-- only a week. Their bodies followed their minds.

For four decades, Langer showed that mental attitude can improve physical health and even reverse effects of aging. Her current research is testing whether metastatic tumors can shrink by similar mental anchoring.

Incidentally, if the above study seems to you as if taken from a Hollywood movie, guess what? The film "*Counter Clockwise*" starring Jennifer Aniston as the young Dr. Langer will be released next year (Pictures, 2017).

To conclude: There is a growing body of evidence that we can influence our minds and hence our actions and our outcomes. This has great implications especially for aging people or for those who are facing any kind of serious illness.

4th Question:
Can we influence our mind only by active means (such as by acting as if we are 20 years younger)? Or can a passive anchor bias our future thoughts as well?

Passive influences are also able to bias your feelings or future decisions. Yale University psychologists Williams and Bargh demonstrated in 2008 that experiencing physical temperature per se (hot or cold drink as an anchor) can affect one's first impressions of individuals when it comes to personality traits. Subjects judged a target person as more generous (as having a warm personality, caring, kind) if they had just held a warm cup of coffee in their hands prior to meeting that target person. And vice versa. (Williams, 2008). The researchers conducted another study showing the power of the warm-cold priming. Another group of 53 participants was asked to briefly hold either a hot pad or a cold pad in order to rate the effectiveness of either stimulus. Later they were given a choice of rewards for participating in the study. Participants could either give a gift to *"a friend,"* or receive it themselves. Participants who evaluated the hot pad were more likely to choose the interpersonally warmer option of a reward for a friend. Those who just held something cold were more likely take something for themselves.

It has been suggested that the insula, a region deep in the cerebral cortex, which plays a role in both the sensation of one's physiological state (such as skin temperature) and the feeling of trustworthiness of others, may account for these findings (Meyer-Lindenberg A., 2008), (Kang Y, 2011).

To conclude: Passively preconditioning our mind may have a similarly positive influence on our brain.

5th Question:
Can preconditioning of our mind have negative as well as positive effects? Will negative thoughts/beliefs result in adverse outcomes?

Both placebo and nocebo are inert substances without any medical effects yet they can benefit (placebo) or worsen (nocebo) the patient's health due to the patient's belief that the substance is effective. Placebo provokes perceived benefits, whereas nocebo is an inert substance, which causes perceived harm (Chavarria V, 2017). The placebo is widely used in clinical trials as a control group to study new treatments. Placebo is commonly used in most of the psychiatric conditions including depression, anxiety, addictions, and even schizophrenia.

The most useful placebo effect occurs in analgesia, or pain control. Decades of study have shown how a psychological expectation triggers neurobiological phenomena in the dorsolateral prefrontal cortex, the anterior cingulate cortex, the amygdala and the periaqueductal gray (Enck, 2013). Placebo is a self-fulfilling prophecy in which positive thoughts, beliefs, and attitude can result in benefit.

On the other end of the scale is the nocebo, a negative self-fulfilling prophecy. Here is one example of how a negative belief can influence people based upon their culture. In Chinese, the number 4 is pronounced "*Si*", the same as the word "*death*" or "*deceased*". Therefore it is a disliked number, much like 13 in the western world. (Henrich, 2015). David Phillips reviewed the death records for the years 1973-1998 of Americans residing in California. There were 209,908 deaths among persons of Asian origin (Chinese and Japanese) and 47,328,762 among Caucasian Americans. He showed that deaths from heart disease were 27 percent higher on the 4th day of all months for people of Asian descent. No similar pattern was found among Caucasian Americans. Phillips titled his article: "*The Hound of the Baskervilles effect: natural experiment on the influence of psychological stress on timing of death*", an allusion to the fatal heart attack of Charles

Baskerville from extreme psychological stress in Sir Arthur Conan Doyle's Sherlock Holmes mystery (Phillips D., 2001).

To conclude: Yes, we can affect outcomes by priming our brain with positive or negative anchors and the self-fulfilling prophecy will always be in the same direction (positive/negative).

6th Question:
What physiological effects are associated with negative and positive emotions? Can it be that positive emotions open our mind? Physiologically widen our view?

Based on her studies, Dr. Barbara Fredrickson stated that positive emotions open our minds. To understand it we will start with the opposite condition.

In 1915 Walter Bradford Cannon, chairman of the Physiology Department at Harvard Medical School, coined the term *"fight-or-flight response"*, also known as acute stress response or hyper arousal. Fight-or-flight is a physiological reaction that occurs in response to a life-threatening event (a real one or a perceived harmful event, attack, or threat to survival). The body's cascade reaction to such a threat will create a boost of energy that prepares the animal for fighting or fleeing. This boost of energy is activated by epinephrine and cortisol. Effect include increases in blood pressure, heart rate, blood sugars, and fats in order to supply the body with extra energy, dilation of the pupil to improve vision, increased blood clotting to reduce excessive blood loss and increased muscle tension.

Easterbrook proposed in 1959 that negative states and particularly high arousal fear or anxiety narrow the scope of attention, obscuring the wide view and making people miss the forest for the trees. Negative emotions prompt a physiological process that narrows a person's momentary thought–action range to promote quick and decisive action. This results in a loss of peripheral vision (tunnel vision), a loss of some hearing, slowing down of the digestive activity and inhibition of erection.

This is in contrast to positive emotions. Barbara Fredrickson from Ann Arbor Michigan argued in her work from 2004 that people should cultivate positive emotions in themselves and in those around them. She advised this not just for the immediate benefit of optimal well-being but also for the promising long-term effects. Positive attitude, she emphasized, is a means to achieving growth and improved physical well-being over time.

Her *"broaden-and-build"* theory suggests that positive emotions physiologically broaden one's awareness and scope of attention and encourage original thoughts and actions (Fredrickson B. L., 2004). When someone has a positive attitude and experiences positive emotions like joy and love, s/he will see more possibilities in their life and will build new skills and develop new resources. Children have been shown to perform better on tests if they had a positive experience prior to the test (like thinking about a positive event in the last year).

The key hypotheses of the *"broaden-and-build"* theory have received empirical support from multiple studies. Participants who were preconditioned with a positive emotion (induced positive emotions by watching cartoons, getting a gift or listening to pleasant music) viewed geometrical figures differently compared to a control group. Preconditioned participants were much more prone to see the big picture, noting more details and more similarity of the figures (Fredrickson BL, 2005). Tracking of subjects' eye movement confirmed that preconditioning with positive emotions resulted in a wider field of view. Subjects who were not preconditioned were less curious and looked only at the center. Viewing more allows you to recognize more possibilities and become more creative; enabling you to bounce back faster from adversity and have more hope (Fredrickson B., 2011).

To conclude: Positive emotions expand your perspective by widening the scope of attention and increasing the peripheral vision. People who cultivate a positive mindset may look around and take in more information, see more possibilities, perform better in the face of challenge and be more likely take advantage of opportunities.

7th Question:
If PMA is that good, how can we rewire our brain to increase positivity, reduce negative thoughts and get even more out of life?

We all know things that enhance our good feelings and create a positive attitude. Among others are mindfulness, meditation, love, sleep, eating, gratitude, optimism, interest, volunteering, writing, exercising, playing, reading self-help books, reading inspiring biographies, smiling, focused breathing, praying and donating.

What is the best way to influence our brain to create the benefits of a positive emotion? We will test this question and choose the best messenger to create positive emotions under the Dobzhansky dictum that *"nothing in biology makes sense except in the light of evolution"* (Carter, 2013).

In evolution, the basic need is to survive. If we die, there is no evolution, that's it. Surviving per Maslow's hierarchy of needs is by meeting basic physiological activities (breathing, basic nutrition such as food and water, homeostasis and excretion, sleep and sex) and by having a safe environment (security of the body, the family, shelter, property, and basic health). Only once individuals have met the basic needs of physiology and safety can they attempt to accomplish more. Therefore, traits that assist in surviving are the most important for evolution.

Love is the first trait that enables survival both when we are young and when we are old. Going back to the evolutionary dictum, without love and the nurturing behavior it fosters, newborns would not survive the first few years. If we have children and none of them survive long enough to reproduce, it is an evolutionary failure. Parental care and support is necessary not only for physical survival and safety but also important for mental health (Carter, 2013). Human experiments have shown in addition that love and the love hormone oxytocin can facilitate our social behavior, including eye contact and social cognition, which helps in meeting our second basic need of a safe environment (Meyer-Lindenberg A. D., 2011).

Similarly, love nourishes us back. Love can boost our immune system and decrease anxiety and depression (Selhub, 2009), whereas stress and loneliness may impair one's immune system and elevate the risk of diseases (Cole Steve W, 2007). Married men with cardiac disease have experienced less myocardial angina if they felt loved by their spouses, despite high-risk factors (cholesterol, diabetes and high blood pressure) (Ornish, 1998).

Thus love has an evolutionary benefit. Feeling secure in your life and in your environment is another basic human need. To increase our chance to survive in an environment threatened by predators or thieves, we live in groups or tribes and respect laws that we create for our mutual protection. Therefore, as with love, being part of a society and strengthening the society should be our goal. It is an evolutionary necessity.

Contributing to creating a stronger and better society can be accomplished by small acts of kindness, being a Good Samaritan, being humble and polite, volunteering one's time for the community, by saving, improving oneself, and even by recycling. The benefit of giving was well known in biblical days.

> *"Give and it will be given to you: good measure, pressed down, shaken together and running over, will be given to you. For with the same measure you measure it will be measured back to you".*
>
> — Luke 6:38

Indeed, the benefits of volunteering are not limited to the recipients (Service, 2007). Volunteers themselves gain a sense of purpose, life satisfaction, and even lower mortality rates. People with a sense of purpose and contribution were found to have favorable gene-expression profiles whereas hedonic well-being has shown no health benefit (Marchant, 2013).

To conclude: To induce positive mental attitude, cultivate love and contribution. Both traits have evolutionary benefits.

Conclusion:

Science has proved time and again that our mental attitude can influence our thoughts, feelings, actions and results. Even more fascinating, it is possible to condition and prime our mental attitude to create a more optimistic mindset, thus fostering more favorable daily outcomes. Even passively preconditioning (listening to music, watching picture of our beloved child or nephew or just having a treat) can positively influence our brains. Priming our brain with a positive anchor works like a self-fulfilling prophecy often leading to better results. Physiologic advantages associated with a positive mindset, such as broader field of vision, may allow the person with a positive mental attitude to deal with challenges in a more holistic fashion.

Viktor Frankl stated that:

> *"Everything can be taken from a man but one thing: the last of the human freedoms; to choose one's attitude in any given set of circumstances, to choose one's own way."*

Bibliography

1959 events. (n.d.). Retrieved from http://www.thepeoplehistory.com/1959.html

Anchoring Wikipedia. (n.d.). Retrieved from https://en.wikipedia.org/wiki/Anchoring

Andrew. (2015, March 9). Criticism of Ellen Langer work. Retrieved from Statistical Modeling, Causal Inference, and Social Science: http://andrewgelman.com/2015/03/09/ellen-langer-expert-victim-illusion-control/

Chavarria V, V. J.-F. (2017). The Placebo and Nocebo Phenomena: Their Clinical Management and Impact on Treatment Outcomes. Clinical Therapeutics, 39(3), 477-486. doi: http://dx.doi.org/10.1016/j.clinthera.2017.01.031

Coyne J., P. (2014, November 5). Re-examining Ellen Langer's classic study of giving plants to nursing home residents. Retrieved from Alternative medicine, cancer, PLOS One commentary: http://blogs.plos.org/mindthebrain/2014/11/05/re-examining-ellen-langers-classic-study-giving-plants-nursing-home-residents/

Enck, P. B. (2013). The placebo response in medicine: minimize, maximize or personalize?. Nat Rev Drug Discov, 12, 191–204.

Fredrickson, B. L. (2004). The broaden-and-build theory of positive emotions. 1367–1378. Retrieved from https://www.ncbi.nlm.nih.gov/pmc/articles/PMC1693418/

Grienson, B. (2014, October 22). https://www.nytimes.com/2014/10/26/magazine/what-if-age-is-nothing-but-a-mind-set.html?_r=2. Retrieved from NY Times: https://www.nytimes.com/2014/10/26/magazine/what-if-age-is-nothing-but-a-mind-set.html?_r=2

Henrich, J. (2015). The Secret of Our Success: How Culture Is Driving Human Evolution, Domesticating Our Species, and Making Us Smarter. Woodstock: Princeton University Press. Retrieved from https://www.amazon.com/Secret-Our-Success-Evolution-Domesticating/dp/0691166854

Kang Y, W. L. (2011). Physical temperature effects on trust behavior: the role of the insula. Soc Cogn Affect Neurosci., 507-515. Retrieved from https://www.ncbi.nlm.nih.gov/pmc/articles/PMC3150863/

Langer, E. J. (1976). The effects of choice and enhanced personal responsibility for the aged: A field experiment in an institutional setting. Jurnal of Personalities and Social Psychology, 34(No 2), 191-198. Retrieved from https://www.researchgate.net/publication/22144050_The_effects_of_c hoice_and_enhanced_personal_responsibility_for_the_aged_A_field_e xperiment_in_an_institutional_setting

Langer, E. J. (2009). Counterclockwise: Mindful Health and the Power of Possibility. New York: Ballantine Books. Retrieved from https://www.amazon.com/Counterclockwise-Mindful-Health-Power-Possibility/dp/0345502043/ref=pd_sim_14_2?_encoding=UTF8&pd_r d_i=0345502043&pd_rd_r=NCVAQHGSTZCZNEJTGFCK&pd_r d_w=sDDBp&pd_rd_wg=rrolC&psc=1&refRID=NCVAQHGSTZC ZNEJTGFCK

Meyer-Lindenberg, A. (2008). Psychology. Trust me on this. Science, 778-780.

Nobel Prize, O. (2002). Nobel Prizes and Laureates 2002 Prize in Economic Sciences. Retrieved from www.nobelprize.org/nobel_prizes/economic-sciences/laureates/2002/

Phillips D., G. C. (2001). The Hound of the Baskervilles effect: natural experiment on the influence of psychological stress on timing of death. BMJ, 323, 1443–1446. Retrieved from https://www.ncbi.nlm.nih.gov/pmc/articles/PMC61045/

Pictures, U. (Director). (2017). Counter Clockwise [Motion Picture]. Retrieved from https://www.movieinsider.com/m3836/counter-clockwise#plot

Tversky Amos, K. D. (1974). Judgment under Uncertainty: Heuristics and Biases. Science, New Series, Vol. 185, No. 4157. (Sep. 27, 1974), pp. 1124-1131., http://links.jstor.org/sici?sici=0036-8075%2819740927%293%3A185%3A4157%3C1124%3AJUUHAB% 3E2.0.CO%3B2-M.

Williams, L. E. (2008). Experiencing Physical Warmth Promotes Interpersonal Warmth. Science, 322, 606-607. Retrieved from https://www.ncbi.nlm.nih.gov/pmc/articles/PMC2737341/

BIO | Tamara Tilleman

A Board Certified Plastic Surgeon and Dean of a Medical School who has devoted considerable research to paradigms and their unconscious influences on decision making and personal and organizational success.

Per her studies paradigm perspectives define one's reality. Not only they affect the way one see the world but they can also replace the reality to the extent that people feel confident that their interpretation is the objective reality.

Her two innovative training programs: "*Successier™*" and "*Leadership without Paradigms™*" are based on her Paradigm Research in the Netherlands and the United States, at Harvard, Maastricht and Erasmus Universities. The workshops' mission is to deliver valuable skills empowering people and organizations to take control over their performances and become successier™.

To schedule keynotes or workshops, please call our customer service: 212-505-0055.

CHAPTER 2

My Journey Through a Dream
By: Brianna M. Lyons, MPH

Daylight proves that no matter the clouds or the rain, the ability to shine still remains. You will always know day from night no matter how many physical obstacles attempt to hinder the sun, it may not always be a clear blue sky but the sun still accomplishes it goal, the rooster crows, you arise from rest, brew your coffee and execute your plan for the day. This is how positive mental attitude works, it is always there it has always existed but it is your choice whether or not to remain activated in the midst of life's storms.

Dreams or Fantasy

Is there truly a difference or are they one in the same. I have experienced first-hand their extremely stark difference. As a child growing up, I had faith but I was very realistic, and although I was an accelerated A student this got me into trouble. In 1st grade at the first report card conference my teacher had nothing but wonderful things to say about me to my parents, most of what they expected until she said well there is one thing… If my mother retells the story you can see in her face the same puzzling look I am certain she gave the teacher because no one had ever had anything but good things to say (not to brag just a testament to the nurturing environment I was raised in) but my teacher said, Brianna does not enjoy fantasy writing and that is a part of our creative writing area, she just does not like it. My mother with a sign of relief as I hadn't actually done something wrong has a slight laugh here because she knew her child. Stories of unicorns and fairy tales just were not my thing. So she asked my teacher, "Is her writing grammatically correct, complete, and unified?" to which she replied yes she does write beautifully. After that meeting my mother asked me about this fantasy/creative writing and I told her, "I am not writing about things that don't exist or have yet to be created." Yes I was that child, I read encyclopedias, I asked teacher for old textbooks to learn over the summer, I even went to writing intensives during the summer. I could create masterfully a story and glean into the future based on present actuality. I was certain that this would not stop me from being great. So she then asked me about dreams and daydreaming and I had an easy and quick answer for that I dreamed all the time. I would dream about eating twin lobsters like I did when we went to Mystic Seaport in Connecticut, about using my skates instead of walking home when my dad picked me up from the bus, about summer and family vacations, and even about having a career and family of my own. I could even make believe, I could dress up like a doctor, lawyer, or veterinarian like a singer, dancer or actor. I would constantly put on shows for my baby dolls, take care of the wounds of my stuffed animals and make my friends my ill patients who needed a doctor for their recovery.

Fantasy should not actually be synonymous with make-believe because it is of utmost importance that you make believe, I mean let's just break down the two words, make and believe. To make something is to develop or create it and to believe is to accept something as true therefore we have created something to accept as truth. The unconscious mind is forced to believe that which it is told. Your conscious thoughts, statements, and actions are automatically accepted by your unconscious mind. This is why people always say be careful what you listen to, what you internalize because it will become a part of your life. I have many friends who played make-believe doctors, lawyers and nurses and they have made that their reality and are successful in those professions today. Make believe gives you the starting point to a roadmap of reality. From make-believe your ability to dream is ignited because you place all of your desires in your dreams, leaving nothing to chance.

Dreams Deferred or Dreams Denied

Now as a grown woman I can really put this into perspective. I always have and always will be a dreamer but I really do not want any parts of fantasy. A dream by definition is a succession of images, thoughts, or emotions passing through the mind during sleep. My personal definition of a dream is- the mental acquisition of a physical reality. You must dream but more importantly you must turn your dreams into reality. Here is where the clouds, the rain, the hurricane, the tornado, the blizzard, the dust bowl come in. When life swirls around you, you must be guided by your Definiteness of Purpose to fulfill the dream that you cannot escape no matter how hard you try, the dream that can keep you up at night and wake you early in the morning. The dream that will force you to make adjustments to the people, places and things in your life. These adjustments will be HARD. These adjustments can cause you to constantly doubt or deny yourself and here lies Positive Mental Attitude. No one ever said making the dream a reality would be easy, it just simply true that it's possible. Anyone who has done something worth remembering fought their way through the storm with Positive Mental Attitude.

Here I am 3,000 miles from home ready to start my sophomore year of college in New Orleans (technically I was a junior from high school college credits) all of my books are purchased and my schedule is perfect. Not even a week of school had passed and there is a Hurricane warning issued. During my freshman year I always ran home only for it to be absolutely nothing so I said I'll just stay we'll be out of school two maybe three days. Well the predicted severity continued to worsen and even locals were packing up to leave town. My friends and I decided we needed to leave too. It took us forever to get out of town even with contraflow, so I decided to use the map to find and follow back roads and we had an interesting trip but we made it to Houston before some people who left before us. Little did we know we had truly dodged a bullet- where we lived during the summer was completely lost to hurricane damage. Hurricane Katrina left it completely underwater, as was the at least the 1st floor of every building at Xavier University of Louisiana. In that moment I found my dreams floating right by, seeming to be a total loss as well. Houston was good to me, I was immediately back to work at The Gap, I enrolled in school (horrible idea- pretty much a waste of time) but all I wanted to do was get back to this new found second home of New Orleans once an official announcement was made that school would reopen in January 2006. I didn't go back home to NY because I didn't want to get stuck, I could handle four months in Texas and hopefully dry out my dreams.

Little did I know that road would be a little bit harder than originally anticipated. I returned to New Orleans in January certain that anything I left in my summer residence was gone but happy to know my dorm room on the 6th floor was not affected by wind damage and the majority of my possessions would be there. Oh but that was not the case, somehow someone thought it would be better to leave the door unlocked because people probably wouldn't have their keys. I went to my room and none of my things were there. What is happening, Positive Mental Attitude out the window I have nothing even though it should've been relatively safe there? I go to the front desk where I am then told oh your stuff should be in the University Center it was reported that you were not coming back to school and in fact your room has been given to someone else (glimmer of Positive Mental Attitude returning, NOPE shot right back down). I was furious, sad, and confused in that moment-should I just go home and sit out and find a school in NY to go to, should I fight for a room even with the lower floors being damaged and there being really no rooms available? I don't know yet but let me go collect my things. Here I am walking to the UC regaining my Positive Mental Attitude, at least I have things to pick up. I enter the room of what looks like a sea of junk and doohickeys. I finally find my things but of course not all of them. All of my Jordan's are gone, some of my jewelry is gone, and again my Positive Mental Attitude is gone (remember I am 19, possessions were important then especially when I worked for what I purchased and took good care of it). There was one good thing my desktop computer was there so I had all of my work, creative projects, and photos back. Now on to find somewhere to live in a hurricane damaged city. I end up living with a group of displaced people and there is not enough room for all of us, our stuff, our hurts and our frustrations. This leads to a near fight one day as someone threatens to throw my stuff in the street to which I in turn threaten that theirs will follow. We go to our respective corners and calm down but it is time to move. Great news I can just move around the corner some apartments have been renovated. I begin moving, driving things back and forth because I didn't have a dolly and on my last trip I have the new puppy I got as a gift with me. I bring some things up the stairs and come back to the car to drive around the corner and sleep for the night the future is looking bright again Positive Mental Attitude and me are friends. I get in the car to go back around the corner only to become a potential casualty to cross car/cab/street gun battle I pull the car over and get down holding my dog probably nearly squeezing her to death until someone says it's safe for you to get out now. This can't be real is what I am saying but it is.

After that random incident (this area didn't/doesn't regularly see this type of crime) things are going well and school is going great I even got to study abroad in Australia but then....things went completely left. My dog was taken and I had to pay to get her back as if she was missing and I was paying a reward, the landlord became unhelpful and questionable people were around too often so it was time to move. I found a great shotgun home in the Mid-City area and I thought perfect, closer to school and work and away from shady characters, little did I know there too would be some pain felt here too. The end of a relationship, an attempted break in and an actual break-in leaving my house in complete chaos -stealing my desktop computer that I discussed earlier and my camera with all of my pictures from Australia but strangely enough none of the TVs or appliances. Not to mention that three days before Mardi Gras 2008 I was in a car accident leaving my car a total loss. All of this, while still working part-time to full time hours now with two jobs, work-study on campus and a full course load. I still graduated on time in May 2008 cum laude with dual minors and dual honors. While I called this grace and dedication, it was in fact Positive Mental Attitude in action along with grace the entire time. I had to find the positive in all of those situations to be where I am today. So the only way my dream could have been denied was if I had chosen to give up the dream and give up the fight, which I never did. I took some hits, some losses but they reconditioned my mind to become stronger mentally and spiritually than a temporary physical situation.

Activation or recovery

You cannot gain PMA from someone else, just like you cannot be motivated by someone else. If you are you will be very limited because you will be negative and unmotivated anytime they are not around. You should always be inspired by someone else as there will always be someone ahead of you in this thing we call life whether it be personal or professional and you can learn from their rain when you may need an umbrella.

Living in a place of positivity and happiness does wonders for every area of your life. Studying is easier, relationships are easier, and getting up every day is easier when your outlook is bright. I was in a new relationship, new job, and beginning my Master's degree program. It was wonderful to be surrounded by a different level of adulthood, people beginning families, careers and finding their purpose. I was working at a Level 1 Trauma center on the evening shift (3pm-11pm) so I could go to school full time. I was in the admitting department and worked in several areas (ER, trauma, labor and delivery, ancillary and direct admitting). In completing my job offer I had to submit a hurricane emergency contact and evacuation location, as well as, a hurricane work preference. I had never had to fill out any form like this in the past but this was the hospital, which doesn't close during emergencies. The form simply said two things: activation or recovery. Activation was staying riding out the storm on lockdown in the hospital, while recovery would require your return to work within 24 hours after receiving a call to come back. My first thought was recovery I want to leave when everyone else leaves I AM NOT staying for a storm (especially after seeing the devastation of Hurricane Katrina). I had 72 hours to submit the form so I decided I would take a little more time and think about it. I know myself and if I leave I don't want to have to jump up to come back (I really do not like to rush), I do not have children, I cared about patients every day and I was more than confident of the competency of the entire hospital staff. In 24 hours I had changed my mind I would stay on activation, just get it done and take a break when they call everyone else back. Every day you make this same choice, activation or recovery, will I get up activated in my life or will I have to recovery from my lack of action.

Dreams into Reality

Fortunately, I never had to stay for a storm. My Positive Mental Attitude had continued to grow as my life continued to flourish. Positive Mental Attitude is a force and when you attach it do your life and desires you will manifest everything you ever wanted. My relationship turned to engagement, work was wonderful, and my degree was going great. I finished my dual degree magna cum laude and had a job waiting for me. Now it was time to begin to design my life. I began wedding planning and house hunting. I knew we couldn't stay where we were any longer we had outgrown the community and we didn't own the property. It was getting closer and closer to the wedding but still no house, doubt starting creeping in that there was no way we were going to find what we wanted and at the price we wanted. All of sudden (October 2010) there was information on a new subdivision with homes completed and move in ready. We knew the area was great and we decided we would go check it out. The house was beautiful, great size for a first home and great closing incentives but there was the price…better than most places we had seen but still more than I was really interested in paying so that was it for me. I knew what I wanted but I wasn't going to look anymore-just wait patiently. Two months later that wait had paid off we got a call that the price was dropped and if we were still interested we could proceed. This was exactly what we needed and it was full steam ahead. Of course there were obstacles at every turn: my now husband has a common name so we had to prove who he was and that he wasn't responsible for debts of someone with the same name and that he had no criminal record. We had to call some creditors for honest debts to prove that they were paid and get credit reports updated. None of this was as easy as these sentences were to write but it was worth it and 90 days later we had a home (90 days before the wedding).

    I had the man of my dreams, the house of my dreams, and now the wedding of my dreams. I had the perfect dress, perfect location, perfect honeymoon, perfect guests, perfect gifts even though I got a speeding ticket, it rained during the reception, and my flight was delayed for our honeymoon. I got exactly what I wanted in my house and my wedding, I took those pebbles designed to take me off course and I paved the road. I used this Positive Mental Attitude and integrated Cosmic Habitforce to then design my business and financial life. Sixty days after getting married my husband and I both lost our jobs one week apart. Now if I had never learned about Positive Mental Attitude my entire world could have been destroyed. Finances end friendships and relationships every single day. I was not happy about the situation but it was at this point that I had to remain in activation and really acknowledge that I had allowed someone else, something else to be fully responsible for the life that I chose to live. Now I said this to say that I have passion for the degrees I chose to pursue but I no longer had the passion to only be a step on the ladder to someone else's success but to build my own ladder. I knew that I didn't want my ladder to be contingent on the efforts of others because people aren't always consistent but life and bills are. I went back to two books: *Think and Grow Rich* and *The Law of Success* both by Napoleon Hill. I read them in the past as they were where I learned the 17 principles but anything worth reading is worth reading more than once. I knew that I had Positive Mental Attitude on my side, I knew my Definiteness of Purpose, and I knew Creative Vision had served me well in all areas of my life. I committed to being a student of success and creating the environment to enhance my Positive Mental Attitude. The only way to have faith is to use it. The only way to freedom is to release, the only way to be positive is to remove everything negative, and your life will be greater for it.

Even the night sky is full of light. The moon and stars are still there to guide you, even when it seems dark. Positive Mental Attitude creates that light in your life. It enables you to see things from a different perspective and find the guideposts (moon and stars) in each situation so that you can stay on course and on purpose to fulfill your dreams. Darkness allows you to shine brighter and stand out. Always be proud of your light, allow it to carry you through life and shine on others along the way.

BIO | Brianna M. Lyons, MPH

Brianna M. Lyons, MPH is student of life. She is a Louisiana transplant by way of New York and a serial entrepreneur. She holds a Bachelor's Degree in Biology from Xavier University of Louisiana and a Dual Master's Degree in Epidemiology and Maternal and Child Health and Development from Tulane University School of Public Health and Tropical Medicine. Throughout her life Brianna's passion for writing, reading and research taught her that success is a moving target and brought her to her journey of discovering personal self-development. Brianna's company, Wealth by Design International has a goal to inspire others to design their best life using their greatest asset (the mind), adding positivity to all areas of their life by discovering who they are and who they want to be through self-study and self-development.

You can email Brianna about wealth and life design at wealthbydesignintl@gmail.com

CHAPTER 3

The Business of Life

By: Matthew Vincent Gold

Chapter 1 The Journey of Life

There are 2 important days in your life: the day you were born and the day you discover why you were born. When you were first born you were completely dependent upon your family to take care of your needs. You learn to become more self-reliant as you become older. Going to high school, possibly college and on into the real world. Eventually you will get married, start a family and live the American dream. Life is not always about the destination, but about the person who you become along the process. As you travel down the road of life, what do you pay attention to? The negativity of trash on the street or the beauty of the flowers or singing of the birds? Sometimes you need to stop and smell the roses. On this journey there are two paths: the easy road and the hard one. Which one you go down is up to you. You will meet many people along this journey. Some are casual passers by, others are short-term acquaintances, but some will turn out to be lifelong friendships. Every journey is full of twists and turns. These challenges can either make you bitter or better. If you are fortunate enough to live a long full life will you look back and be satisfied with what you accomplished? About all the lives you made a lasting impact on? Everyone leaves a legacy. But the sad truth is the wealthiest place in the world is the graveyard with all the unfulfilled goals and dreams that die with people. I truly hope that doesn't describe you and that you will leave the world a better place because you were in it.

In the words of Gandhi:

> *"Be the change you want to see in the world "*

Chapter 2 The Power of goals

When you traveling on this journey, you need directions otherwise you will be traveling aimlessly. Everyone was born to fulfill a unique purpose. Is your dream to start that business, buy that luxury item or travel the world? Begin with the end in mind and build you plan backwards to where you currently at in life. Let's say your goal is to win the championship. When you do win it will be a great achievement for sure, but then what? Success is always a moving target. Make sure you're constantly readjusting to it. When setting goals a good plan is to use the *SMART* method. It stands for *S*pecific, *M*easurable, *A*chievable, *R*ealistic, and *T*imeline. Make your goals Specific. A specific goal has a greater chance of being achieved than a generic one. To make it specific it must answer the six w questions: who is involved? What do I want to accomplish? Where? Identify a location. When? Establish a timeframe. Which? Identity requirements and constraints. Why? Specific reasons and benefits of accomplishing the goal. Measurable- Establish specific criteria for measuring progress toward the attainment of every goal you set. Measuring your progress helps you stay in course, reach your target dates and experience the thrill of achievement that drives you to continue to your destination. To determine if it is measurable, ask yourself how will you know if it is accomplished? Attainable-Identify goals that are important to you. You will begin to find ways to make them come into reality. You will begin to develop the attitudes, abilities, skills and financing to achieve them you will begin to see opportunities are everywhere around you. No goal is impossible if you establish a time frame to achieve it. Goals that seem too big will become realistic and attainable, because you grow and match them. Realistic-To be realistic, your goals must represent an idea toward you are willing and able to work. Only you can decide how big your goals can be. Big goals are usually easier to achieve because it gives you a strong desire. Hard tasks will seem easy if you do them in a labor of love. Make sure you write out your goals to paper. Visualizing them makes them real and more attainable. Timely- a goal should be limited within a time frame. Time frames create a sense of urgency. It is not enough to say I want more money. How much? When you establish it within a time frame then you've put your subconscious mind into play working to achieve it. If you believe you can achieve it, it is realistic. A goal is tangible if you can experience it with any of the five senses of sight, smell, taste, touch and hearing. This increases your odds of making it specific and measurable, and ultimately attainable.

Chapter 3 Personal Development

Being on your journey and having goals are crucial to your success journey. The best investment you can ever make in life is in growing your mindset. I would say it is a better invest than stocks, real estate or a business. There many great books out there to read. One of my favorites is the 1937 classic by Napoleon Hill *Think and Grow Rich*. In the book he is quoted: "*Whatever the mind of man can conceive and believe, he can achieve*" and "*More gold is farmed from the mind of man than has ever been farmed from the earth*" I first came upon *Think and Grow Rich* in 2002 when I was out of high school, looking for direction in my life. The biggest value I got from the book is the value of having a burning desire backed by a definiteness of purpose. When you look at successful people, I would say they all have this principle. What you know got you where you are. If you want to get to the next level you need to expand your mindset. To master a new skill they say it takes 10,000 hours of consistent practice.

Chapter 4 Teamwork makes the dream work

No man is an island. Nobody wins the championship trophy by himself. When you look at championship teams like the New England patriots and the golden state warriors, you are seeing the finished product. What you don't see is the Years of practice, hard work, blood, sweat and tears that go into it. Every great team rises or falls on its leadership. History has proven that great leaders have achieved success by energizing their followers while recruiting many more simultaneously. You can't expect any great success without the helping hands and minds of other people. Even if you have talent at the level of a Michael Jordan, you need teammates like Scottie Pippen and Dennis Rodman along with the Mentorship of Phil Jackson. Mentorship is extremely important to your success because you can't see the whole picture, when you are inside of the frame. You might be asking, "*Where do I find someone to mentor me?*" Great question. There are lot of people who would give their time me to mentor you, if you seek them out. Make sure they are reputable and have a solid track record. Never seek advice from someone who you wouldn't trade shoes with. You might think that guy is so successful he would never give me the time of day. You never know if you don't ask. And find a way to add value to them. Even if it is going on a coffee run, you never know how that can open doors.

In closing, I hope this has been informative to you. I wish you success on your journey. Always remember the world is constantly changing and you always got to keep changing with it. Here in Austin there are 2 great sayings: "*The pride and winning tradition of the university of Texas will not be entrusted to the weak and timid.*" And "*What starts here, changes the world*"

God bless, Matthew

BIO | Matthew Vincent Gold

Matthew gold is an entrepreneur and author. He has built several successful businesses over the last 12 years and an avid reader of personal development. He is also a big sports fan of the Texas longhorns, Dallas cowboys, Houston Texans and San Antonio spurs.

Contact him on Facebook, Twitter and Instagram @mvg512

CHAPTER 4

How I Built An 8-Figure Company With No Experience (And So Can You)

By: Jeffery Feldberg

Let me ask you something: Can a kid right out of school, with no business experience, build an 8-figure company?

The so-called experts would say not likely at best, and impossible at worst. But from one entrepreneur to another, know this: The correct spelling of 'Impossible' is "I'm Possible." You see, that kid was me. And what did I bring to the table?

The ink was still drying on my MBA degree when I hung up the proverbial shingle and went into business. I had zero business experience. While on the topic of zero, know that my bank account wasn't far off. My competitors were well financed and run by experienced leaders and managers. Despite the odds, not only did I survive, I thrived. If I can do it, so can you.

Congratulations for reading my chapter and this book. Whether you're just starting or looking to get an edge, your well on your way. And great news! In my chapter, I reveal 17 principles that helped me create an 8-figure company otherwise known as Embanet.

Ready? Great, let's do it!

Entrepreneurship Is An Excuse To Solve Problems and Help People

For me, entrepreneurship provides an opportunity to help people and solve problems. The world has entrepreneurs to thank for making life better, safer, and more enjoyable. Take a look around. Your favorite product or service likely came from solving a problem.

I was no different when I launched Embanet, an eLearning company. Even though I sold Embanet after thirteen years of building it into a profit monster, it still exists today!

While I can go into details of what Embanet did, it's not relevant to you. What more important is the knowledge of how I leveraged Napoleon Hill's principles of a Positive Mental Attitude to build Embanet into an 8-figure business.

Each success principle is powerful and can be a chapter unto itself. But the magic happens once you combine these success principles.

To get the most from this chapter, focus on one success principle at a time.

Once you've mastered one principle move on to the next success principle. Be patient and consistent as you're positioning yourself to build your 8-figure company.

Success Principle 1 - Definiteness of Purpose

Success Whisperer Napoleon Hill says it best for Definiteness of Purpose:

> *"There is one quality which one must possess to win, and that is definiteness of purpose, the knowledge of what one wants, and a burning desire to possess it."*

When you don't have a Definiteness of Purpose, you're like a ship without a rudder. And as a result, your schedule and direction in life are not your own. Your agenda is at the whim of those around you.

Having a Definiteness of Purpose helps in two key areas:

1. Keeps you on track for your vision and goals.
2. Helps you decide where to focus your time and attention.

For the sake of brevity, I've edited down my Definiteness of Purpose. My first version when I began Embanet was:

> *"Enable business school faculty and students to learn anywhere at any time."*

Over time my Definiteness of Purpose changed and became:

> *"Embanet helps schools achieve high enrollments, completion rates, and return-on-investment."*

My second Definiteness of Purpose spoke to both my target market and me. Over time I learned that my target market, University Presidents, desired two things. First, a quality online program that had most of the student's graduate. Second, the online program is profitable to the University. As an entrepreneur, it's easy to lose control of your time and focus. My Definiteness of Purpose kept me on track.

When invited to a meeting or I needed to make a difficult decision, I asked myself one question:

> *"Will this activity help me increase enrollments and profits for my customers?" Saying 'yes' to the things that mattered became easy. And as important, if not more necessary, saying 'no' became even easier.*

Creating Your Definiteness of Purpose

Hill's step-by-step method for creating your Definiteness of Purpose is as follows:

1. Determine exactly what you desire. Your desire must be a 'burning desire.' Keep it precise. As an example, saying you want to be rich is vague. Instead, saying you would like to be in possession of a million dollars is specific.
2. Calculate when you'll achieve your desire. If you're not sure, that's OK. Write down your best guess. Remember, don't make the timeline short, but also, don't make it too long.
3. Decide what you'll do to achieve your desire. As the saying goes, you can't get something for nothing. Think about what you will offer or provide for achieving your goal.

4. Map out a plan of the steps you'll take to fulfill your desire. Know that your plan will likely change, but you need to start somewhere.
5. Write out a clear and detailed statement. This statement becomes your Definiteness of Purpose.
6. Read your Definiteness of Purpose upon waking and right before you go to bed. Do this every day.

Whether you're a martial arts fan or not, you've likely heard of the legendary Bruce Lee. As a student of success, Lee created is own definiteness of purpose which reads:

> *I, Bruce Lee, will be the first highest paid Oriental super star in the United States. In return, I will give the most exciting performances and render the best of quality in the capacity of an actor. Starting 1970 I will achieve world fame, and from then onward, till the end of 1980, I will have in my possession $10,000,000. I will live the way I please and achieve inner harmony and happiness.*

Notice how Lee is specific by naming the year he starts to achieve his fame and the year he is in possession of his goal. Speaking of goals, Lee doesn't just say he wants to be rich. Lee specifies the exact figure of $10,000,000.

When creating your definiteness of purpose, be precise and detailed.

Success Principle 2 - The Mastermind

The mastermind term comes from Success Whisperer Napoleon

Hill who defined it as:

> *"A friendly alliance with one or more persons who will encourage one to follow through with both plan and purpose."*

Think of a mastermind group like your personal board of advisors. The only agenda for your mastermind group is your success. Although a mastermind group can be as small as two people, it's ideal to have more. Steel magnate Andrew Carnegie attributes his success to his mastermind group. Carnegie goes down in the history books as one of the most successful businessmen, ever. And for you history buffs, King Arthur and the Knights of the Round Table were a mastermind.

Here's a question for you.

What do The Chronicles of Narnia and The Lord of the Rings have in common? The authors, CS Lewis and JRR Tolkien, were members of the 'Inklings' mastermind.

I've been leveraging the power of mastermind groups for many years now. My best business breakthroughs have come from my mastermind group. One idea was so powerful that it led to a new division at Embanet with a new business partner. This one idea rocketed Embanet into the future. We leapfrogged the competition, solved a major problem for our clients, and profited.

How To Set Up A Mastermind Group

To get the most out of your mastermind group, try the following:

1. Ensure no more than 8 members from different industries
2. No member is a competitor to another member
3. Meet at least once a month

4. Everyone must provide candid and honest feedback while holding you accountable.
5. Meetings are monthly, or more often if required.
6. One member of the group acts as the moderator to ensure the meeting stays on track.
7. Each member of the group presents during the meeting.

There are now many companies and individuals who offer services to put you in a mastermind group, for a fee. Fee or no fee, know that your mastermind group is only as good as the quality of people in the group itself. When it comes to your mastermind group, check your ego at the door. Hopefully, you're NOT the smartest one in the room. If you are, find another mastermind group. Why you ask? When you surround yourself with people who are both smarter and better than you in specific areas, you'll learn. Over time you'll give back to your mastermind group through your unique talents and skills.

Success Principle 3 - Applied Faith

Do you know a four letter 'F' word that is a dream killer?

Ready?

F.E.A.R.

The antidote for fear is applied faith. To realize success and overcome fear entrepreneurs can depend on applied faith. Applied faith is a state of mind in which you believe in yourself, your ability, and that things will work out. Let me be clear. I'm not saying to ignore everything around you, do nothing, and hope for the best. Applied faith on its own will not bring you success. What you will achieve through applied faith is the ability to see what you need to do for success. I started Embanet out of the attic in my parents' home. My team consisted of me, myself and I. I can best summarize the early days in three words.

Painful.

Agonizing.

Lonely.

Many mornings I woke up and was outright scared to take the ten steps to my desk and start my workday. I had more rejection that I care to remember. My friends and family thought I was crazy. Remember, my MBA friends were enjoying six-figure incomes and cushy corporate perks. What got me out of bed, every day was faith. I didn't know how I would do it. All I knew was that I would find a way.

My definiteness of purpose (Success Principle 1) kept me focused. My applied faith was an active mindset that kept me open to the possibility. On paper, I should have failed in every way. Remember, I had no business experience, team, or money. All I had was my burning desire to help people and solve a problem.

How to Invoke Applied Faith

The subconscious mind is incredible. Did you know that your brain couldn't tell the difference between what's real and not? Ever wonder why a movie or a great book can move you to laughter or tears? Your mind can't tell the difference between the film and reality. Applied faith works the same way. What you say to yourself are affirmations that your subconscious mind believes are real.

Here are the steps I took to develop applied faith:

1. With a high level of emotion, I told myself that I have everything I need, right now, to achieve my definite purpose. I felt and saw myself taking constant action to realize my definite purpose.
2. I visualized the person I wanted to be. The vision of myself was clear and bright in my mind.

3. I believed and knew that I would find a way to achieve my desire. I saw myself acting as if I already reached my goal and how it felt.
4. I read my definite purpose with feeling and emotion.
5. I created an active state of mind that either eliminated negative thoughts. Negative thoughts could have come from myself or those around me. Either way, I ensured to find the positive in every situation.

Success Principle 4 - Going The Extra Mile

Going the extra mile is one of those 'small things' that makes all the difference.

Author Og Mandino says it best:

> *"Always render more and better service than is expected of you, no matter what your task may be."*

Going the extra mile does two things:

1. You create a legion of Raving Fans who sing your praise to anyone and everyone
2. Your Raving Fans assist in creating a profitable company.

Let me share a quick story.

> *I was at a trade show for universities and colleges. Lack of money ensured that I did the trip solo. The conference ended at 4 pm. By 2 pm most of the exhibitors, my competition included, called it quits. At 4:15 pm I began to pack up when a gentleman walked up with questions. For the next hour, I answered every question the gentleman could think of with a smile. Most of the questions had nothing to do with Embanet.*

A few weeks later I received a phone call from the same gentleman who was the President of a large university. The President appreciated my time and effort. As a result of going the extra mile, I was invited to his campus to speak with his team about online learning. Long story short, the President and the University became a customer; all because I decided to go the extra mile. Going the extra mile costs you nothing but your time and a great attitude. Make it a way of life and do it because you choose to, not because you have to. And while you're at it, when you go the extra mile expect nothing in return. Will you be taken advantage of by going the extra mile? You may. But know this. The joy, opportunity, and difference of going the extra mile far outweigh anything else.

Success Principle 5 - A Pleasing Personality

The difference between winning or losing business comes down Y.O.U. People prefer to do business with people they like. Your personality will either be your biggest asset or liability.

It was Success Principle 5 that launched Embanet. For over a year I was struggling to get my first customer. Although we take it for granted today, the Internet and doing things online was both new and scary. This new thing called the Internet peaked the interest of a business school in the Midwest.

Tired of using video tapes (remember those!?), the Dean of the business school, Jon, was ready to make a change. I will always remember the phone call from Jon. "*Jeffrey*," said Jon excitedly; I've decided to go with Embanet to make the switch to online learning. Let's be honest. You don't have any track record to speak of, and you look like you're still in high school. Despite this, I like you and know that you'll do whatever it takes to ensure my program is a success. Send me your contract and let me know when we can start". A pleasing personality made all the difference. Having a pleasant personality cost nothing and makes all the difference.

Success Principle 6 - Personal Initiative

Author extraordinaire Stephen King is right on point when he tells us:

> "*Amateurs just and wait for inspiration, the rest of us just get up and go to work.*"

It's easy to get caught up in procrastination or waiting for that 'perfect' plan. Success Principle 6, personal initiative, is all about taking action N.O.W. Personal initiative is also finishing what you start. Between smartphones and the Internet, we're facing an epidemic of distractions. I was shocked when I learned that the average workday presents 60 or more distractions. As if this isn't challenging enough, every time you're distracted it takes your brain 23 minutes to get back into state. So, how do maximize your time and results? Unfortunately, it's too easy to confuse activity with progress. As important as taking the initiative is knowing when to say 'no.' When I started Embanet, I said 'yes' to everything. I was in experimentation mode. Once I began to get traction and results I said 'no' more than I said 'yes.'

My definite purpose helped me figure out when I should say 'yes.' Do you remember that one simple question to ask?

It's this:

> *"Will this request move me one step closer to achieving my definite purpose?"*

Time, and not money, is your most precious resource. Take action and protect your time. Here are my best practices to ensure I minimize disruptions and maximize my personal initiative:

- My most energetic and productive time for me is first thing in the morning. I do my most important things in the morning. Everyone is different. Your most productive time may be in the evening. Do what works for you.
- The night before or first thing in the morning, I choose the top three to five things I must do. If I don't complete these tasks before the day is out, I continue them the following day.
- During my productive time, I avoid email, social media, phone calls and interruptions. If I'm working in my office, my team knows not to disturb me when my door is closed.
- I avoid email and voice mail. Reading an email may only take seconds, but it can negatively affect my mindset for hours.
- I keep water, snacks and extra supplies at my desk so I'm not interrupting myself to get something.

Why not check out my blog post 'Stop Wasting Time and Skyrocket Success' at jeffreyfeldberg.com where I go into even more detail. You'll learn and prosper!

Success Principle 7 - Positive Mental Attitude

Ralph Waldo Emerson best sums up Success Principle 7 with his quote:

> *"Be careful what you set your heart on,*
> *for it will surely be yours."*

Your attitude is everything. Have the wrong attitude, and you lock out success. **Period. End of story.** Let me illustrate. Suppose you purchased a red sweater. Almost by magic, you start seeing red sweaters everywhere. The day before, these red sweaters were nowhere in sight. What happened? Scientists call this the 'Baader-Meinhof phenomenon.' When you bought the red sweater, it registered with your brain.

When I launched Embanet in 1995, the so-called 'experts' told me I was 'crazy' for relying on the Internet over dial-up modems. The same 'experts' reasoned it's so much easier to take the drive to campus and learn from a live professor. Today these challenges, and not me, sound 'crazy.' But in 1995 things were different.

My positive mental attitude made it so clear and obvious that the Internet was the only way to go. It was also clear that learning in the comfort of your home or office was the ultimate in convenience. I was open to new ideas and ways of doing things. Embanet was more profitable, efficient and productive than its competitors. Why? My positive attitude allowed me to create best practices that met the challenge. The competition and experts laughed and shook their heads. Embanet changed lives. Embanet's customers, the schools, and Embanet had the last laugh, all the way to the bank. Remember, a positive mental attitude has you see the solution where others only see the problem.

Success Principle 8 - Enthusiasm

When it comes to enthusiasm, Success Whisperer Napoleon Hill reminds us:

> *"A man without enthusiasm is like an automobile without gasoline."*

As with Success Principle 7, enthusiasm is a state of mind. Let me bust a myth that has been circulating for too long. People make decisions on emotion first and justify it with logic afterward. Social programming tells you the logic rules. It doesn't. Enthusiasm is contagious.

An entrepreneur without enthusiasm is a failure waiting to happen. From elevating your staff to your customers, your enthusiasm is fuel for you and your company. To be clear, I'm not advocating you pump your fists in the air and thump your chest like a buffoon.

Your definite purpose (Success Principle 1) ensures your enthusiasm is natural. Yes, you'll experience days that are challenging and tough. Your enthusiasm is most important on your difficult days.

In my experience, when I'm feeling down it's my enthusiasm that picks me right back up. And you know what, I rock my day and make a difference. And if you up for the challenge, why not go from enthusiastic to charismatic.

Success Principle 9 - Self Discipline

A lack of self-discipline is like having a car speeding down a hill without any brakes or steering wheel. Self-discipline keeps in check your enthusiasm, personal initiative and positive mental attitude. At Embanet I developed what I now call the 24-hour rule. What is the 24-hour rule? When I hit a milestone or won a new contract, I would celebrate like there's no tomorrow. When I had a setback or defeat, I would feel the pain. But win or lose, tomorrow is a new day filled with opportunities.

How do you develop and maintain self-discipline?

My top 7 hacks for self-discipline that leads to success:

1. Develop daily rituals, that when followed, move you towards achieving your definite purpose.
2. The night before or the morning of, write down the top 3 to 5 tasks to achieve. Remember, if the task doesn't move you closer to your definite purpose, don't do it. Whatever tasks you haven't completed, move them forward to the next day.
3. Build in fun throughout your day and week to keep you refreshed.
4. Accept mistakes and move forward.
5. Know what your 'kryptonite' is and remove it from your working environment. As an example, suppose you spend hours playing 'Trivia Crack.' Eliminate the app from your phone to avoid temptation. If you have a tablet or extra phone at home, play the app on that device when you're not working.
6. Get at least 6 to 8 hours of sleep each night.
7. Eat healthy foods. Whole foods with minimal sugar and processing are preferred.

Success Principle 10 - Accurate Thinking

With the rise of social media and 'fake news,' the habit of accurate thinking couldn't be timelier.

Accurate thinking is the discipline of filtering information into two categories:

1. Important
2. Unimportant

Anything that moves you closer to your definite purpose is important. It's OK and even encouraged to seek information from other people. What's important is that you, and you alone, make the decision. Never let anyone do the thinking for you. At Embanet, accurate thinking played a significant role in becoming an 8-figure company. Embanet set the gold standard in two distinct areas. The first area was online course development. The second area was the marketing and enrollment of students into degree programs. We achieved a fierce competitive advantage that steamrolled over the competition. Embanet also benefited from a healthy bottom line. And the secret to our success in these areas? Embanet defied conventional wisdom and proved the experts wrong, time-and-time again. Embanet was able to do this because of accurate thinking.

Success Principle 11 - Controlled Attention

The power of controlled attention, otherwise known as focus, is best summed up by Bruce Lee:

> *"The successful warrior is the average man, with laser-like focus."*

The numbers say it all, and it isn't pretty. Evan Asano reports in Social Media Today that we consume 116 minutes a day on social media. YouTube clocks in at 40 minutes, Facebook at 35 minutes and Snapchat at 25 minutes. Each. And. Every. Day. On paper, Embanet should have failed. Instead, Embanet became an 8-figure company. Why? Controlled attention, or focus, played a significant role. I had a burning desire for Embanet to succeed through helping working professionals. My goal was to change the social fabric of society, one graduate at a time. I thought about my definite purpose from the moment I woke up until I slept. And many nights I dreamed of achieving my definite purpose. As I mentioned earlier, I said 'no' to the unimportant and 'yes' to the important. As Embanet grew, my ability to focus became difficult as I was pulled in many directions. Finding and hiring the right people helped.

But know this.

Controlled attention is two things:

1. Focus your mind on what you want and believe it will happen.
2. Don't focus on the thing you don't want.

As simple as this principle sounds, in practice this is challenging. Master this principle, and you become a master of your thoughts and destiny.

Success Principle 12 - Teamwork

Behind every success story is a team that made it happen. As Michael Jordan says:

> "Talent wins games, but teamwork and intelligence win championships."

Embanet was no exception. As business grew and the demands on my time did the same, I knew that my future success depended on hiring right. My goal was to fire myself through hiring people who could replace me. I also mastered the art of delegation. It was a great feeling knowing that a smarter and more talented person was getting things done. Teamwork is all about the right people. Always be on the lookout for talented people that can become part of your team.

Success Principle 13 - Learning from Adversity and Defeat

Having achieved massive success, I learned many valuable lessons. One of the most valuable is this: If you're not failing, you're not trying hard enough. Contrary to popular belief, failure is your friend. My biggest success has happened right after my biggest failure. It's only through failure that you become better and more prepared. Looking back now, I can see that I was not ready for the success that was waiting for me. As bizarre as this may sound, I needed to fail before I could succeed. To understand why, go to jeffreyfeldberg.com and read my blog post, '*How to Welcome Failure For Spectacular Success.*'

As much as so-called failure hurts, know that you're one step closer to success. Below are ten questions that transform failure into success:

1. How did this happen?
2. Looking back, what could I change that would have led to a better outcome?
3. Is there anything I can do right now to turn the situation around?
4. Who can I turn to for an outsider's perspective on my failure?
5. What assumptions did I make and were they right?
6. When could I have changed to avoid failure?
7. If I could do it all over again, what would I do and not do?
8. What have I learned from this situation?
9. Going forward, how will I prevent this failure from happening again?
10. Who can help identify blind spots in my thinking, assumptions, and behavior? Select someone who knows you well.

In closing, know this. Failure is your best teacher. Learn to master how you both deal with and learn from failure and the future is yours.

Success Principle 14 - Creative Vision

Here's a question for you. What do Richard Branson, Warren Buffett, and Bill Gates have in common? Branson, Buffett, and Gates make it a point to think big. Embanet became an 8-figure company because of creative vision. In the beginning, Embanet's focus was hosting, course development and technical support. The creative vision led Embanet to take on marketing and student enrollments. The same creative vision changed up our business model. These two changes catapulted Embanet to an even greater level of success in every way. When I led Embanet, our vision was to change the social fabric of society. To do this, we pictured Embanet becoming the 'operating software' of the industry.

Norman Vincent Peale said it best through his book *The Power of Positive Thinking*:

> *"Shoot for the moon. Even if you miss, you'll land among the stars."*

What are you waiting for?!

Success Principle 15 - Maintenance of Sound Health

When it comes to health I can say it no better than the wise, but unknown soul, who once said:

> *"The greatest wealth is health."*

I discovered the perfect recipe for being unhealthy. Combine too many plane rides, not enough home cooked meals and lack of exercise. The thought of lacking energy, having a body that aches and brain fog make me shudder.

Never again.

I've since become vigilant on my health. I watch what I eat, sleep 6 to 8 hours a night, and enjoy a moderate amount of exercise. Although this takes time and effort, I've noticed a huge difference. With so many resources available on what to eat and how to exercise, I encourage you to try it for yourself. Whatever doesn't work, toss. Whatever makes you feel great, keep. But know this. Your business success will falter if your health falters. Take care of your body, and it will take care of you.

Success Principle 16 - Budgeting Time and Money

While both time and money are important, your most vital resource is your time. From a billionaire to someone who's broke, everyone has 1,440 minutes every day.

No more. No less.

Each of the Success Principles I've talked about performed like a symphony. One principle built upon the other. From the lack of money, I learned the power of knowledge and what to do with it.

Being able to write the check doesn't mean you should. Embanet couldn't write the check. Instead, time was the currency used to master the process and hack the system. Despite having a lot of time, I had a sense of urgency. I didn't put things off to the future.

In Embanet's early years, we lacked discipline around time. We did not differentiate the urgent from the important. It wasn't pleasant. That said, this all changed with the mastery of budgeting time and money.

When Embanet began to grow, I never forgot my humble beginnings. When Embanet had profits, I still ran the company as though funds were scarce. As a result, our efficiency and cost effectiveness were one of the best in the industry. It wasn't easy. As an example, when traveling, it was two people to a hotel room.

No exceptions. Myself included. Making a trip in a day, even a long day, was preferred to the cost of staying overnight. And when it came to time, the joke with the Embanet team was that one month for us was like three months for everyone else. Despite the sacrifices, Embanet's culture thrived. Our customers were profitable, as was Embanet.

Success Principle 17 - Cosmic Habitforce

Napoleon Hill coined the term 'Cosmic Habitforce.' What's a cosmic habit force, you ask? Great question.

Who better to answer this than Napoleon Hill himself, who said:

> *"Man is not bound by instinct; man is bound only by the imagination and the willpower of his own mind."*

And building upon the last quote is another quote from Hill, which seals the deal:

> *"What the mind can conceive and believe, it can achieve."*

It was no different for me. In my mind, I imagined and felt what it was like for Embanet to change the social fabric of society, one graduate at a time. My entire outlook focused on Embanet succeeding. In my mind, failure was not a possibility. Every time I experienced a challenge or difficulty with Embanet, I looked for the lesson. I challenged myself to find a better way. I would not take 'no' for an answer. Is this to say that everything worked out as I desired? Of course not. Despite the setbacks, I took great comfort in knowing I would find a way even if I couldn't see it. And isn't this what life and business are all about? Being an entrepreneur is an act of pure faith. From the depths of the great unknown have come solutions to humanity's problems. If being an entrepreneur is an excuse to solve problems, then cosmic habit force is the way to solve those problems. With this in mind, it's only appropriate to close out this Success Principle the same way we started it.

> *"What the mind can conceive and believe, it can achieve."*
>
> — Napoleon Hill

It Worked For Me, And You Can Do The Same

If can build an 8-figure company with no experience and money, so can you.

I found a massive problem that I was passionate to solve. In my case, I did the following:

1. Helped universities recruit quality students into online degree program.
2. Keep the students in their seats once they enrolled in their program. Average completion rates before Embanet arrived on the scene was 60% on a good day. With Embanet, completion rates were as high as 93.8%.
3. Ensured Embanet's partners, the universities, were profitable. And were they ever!

When I started Embanet, it was out of my room in my parents' attic. Thirteen years later Embanet was in it's own building and had nearly 200 employees. My definite purpose of changing the social fabric of society, one graduate at a time, became a reality.

Embanet was privileged to help enroll:

- Presidents of Fortune 100 companies

- High ranking government officials
- Law enforcement professionals
- Single mothers.

The one thing in common for the students was the desire to change their lives for the better through education. My business partners and I achieved this over thirteen years. It was a great ride that was fulfilling and life changing. It was not an easy decision to sell Embanet. My baby had grown from nothing into an 8-figure company that dominated the industry. But it was time. My passion is solving problems and creating. It's the same for my business partners. Embanet required a different leadership style to continue to grow and prosper. Two venture capital groups teamed up and purchased Embanet. This same group later sold Embanet to Pearson Publishing; and all of this from 17 Success Principles and a kid with no business experience.

Conclusion

On paper, my first venture out of school, Embanet, should have been a spectacular failure.

Think about it. I had zero business experience. There was little to no money. I lacked a team; let alone seasoned business executives. All I had was an idea and a passion for solving a problem and helping people.

So how is it that kid, aka yours truly, built a successful and profitable 8-figure company on his first try? Sounds too good to be true, or like a storyline right out of Hollywood? The truth is stranger than fiction. Could you say that I was lucky and was at the right place at the right time? Glad you asked! I believe the harder I work the 'luckier' I become. Am I some genius who has a unique ability? Yeah, right! That would be nice. I'm no different than you. In fact, if I had a dollar for every mistake I made, it would be larger than what I amassed! So what was my 'secret'? You already know my so-called secret. It's the 17 Success Principles I've shared in this chapter. Each Success Principle on its own makes a difference. Combine all 17, and you command success.

Whether you're starting out or you're looking to grow your existing business, know your future success is waiting for you. These 17 Success Principles will be your guide and your way.

So what are you waiting for? Here's to you and your success!

In Thanks and Gratitude,

Jeffrey Feldberg

P.S. Congratulations on completing my chapter! As a thank you, I've arranged a VIP success package for you at www.jeffreyfeldberg.com/thankyou

BIO | Jeffrey Feldberg

Like you, entrepreneur and thought leader Jeffrey Feldberg cheers entrepreneurs who change society.

With over two decades of real-life experience, Jeffrey's view is different and intriguing. Most important, Jeffrey has real-life, in-the-trenches experience of building an 8-figure business.

The motto: '*Your Success. My Obsession.*' is the driving force for Jeffrey to help entrepreneurs change the world.

As a best-selling author and blogger, Jeffrey shares principles that get results. Jeffrey blends his in-the-trenches business stories with his story telling ability.

Through his coaching, Jeffrey brings out the best in you with his candid, yet caring manner.

As a best-selling author and blogger, Jeffrey shares principles that get results. Jeffrey blends his in-the-trenches business stories with his story telling ability.

Through his coaching, Jeffrey brings out the best in you with his candid, yet caring manner.

Interested in speaking with Jeffrey? You can reach Jeffrey and receive a personal reply from him through:

hello@jeffreyfeldberg.com

CHAPTER 5

I Don't Paint Rust Anymore

By: Scott Venezia

Where is Everything?

*"Mom, I don't want to go home now.
I'm not done playing!"*

I whined unsuccessfully.

I remember very well that warm, humid summer day in 1971. I was only six years old at the time, so I'm not too sure I knew what humid was. But, I do remember how hot and sticky and gross I felt. That's what all the summers in Buffalo, NY felt like to everyone – hot, sticky, and gross.

Mom and I had just spent the day at grandma's eating hot dogs, hamburgers, and corn on the cob. Dad didn't come with us because he had other things to do, which was most of the time. So, the two of us enjoyed the day with grandma and my step-grandfather.

I was running around, playing most of the day, as any rambunctious six-year-old would. So, I was extra sweaty by the time we had to leave. Mom yelled, *"Charlie, get in the car!"* that's what she called me when I was in trouble. I don't know where that name came from, but I knew when I heard it, mom meant business. *"We have to get you into the bath, let's go."* she added. We said our goodbyes with hugs and kisses and mom corralled me into our rusted out '61 Chevrolet Bel Air and off we went.

I loved that car because I got to help mom and grandma paint it in the parking lot of Riverside Park. We were armed with a few cans of dark blue paint and three paint brushes, and we went to work. It took most of the afternoon for the three of us to paint the car. I felt special because I got to paint all of the rust spots! It looked beautiful. At least that's what my six-year-old self remembers, so we'll stick with that.

Mom drove us the two blocks to get home. She said it was too hot to be walking even one block. It didn't make sense to me; I walked to grandma's house all the time in the summer!

After mom had parked the car, I shuffled out of the back seat. I trailed behind my mother, like any dutiful child would, up the long sidewalk and to the door of our apartment. We lived in the end unit of the government housing building at Kenmore and Grove. The "*projects*" was our home for nearly two years.

Little did I know my life was about to change the instant mom opened the door.

I can picture it clear as day and it's all in slow motion. Mom put the key in the lock, turned it and opened the door. That very instant mom let out a thunderous expletive, *"What the f$%@!"* I didn't know whether to be scared or excited. So, I nudged my way around mom to see what was going on. I just stood in the kitchen in disbelief. There was nothing downstairs but the kitchen table - no living room furniture, no television, no washer or dryer. Even the refrigerator was gone. Nothing was left but the seemingly lonely kitchen table.

I quickly left mom behind and ran upstairs to see if there was anything left in my room. All my toys were still scattered around the room and in the corner, against the white brick wall, was my bed. That's it. Mom was crying and yelling things I don't remember, as she reached the top step. We both walked into her room together and saw that her bedroom was empty too. Just like downstairs, nothing but bare walls.

Mom stood in the middle of her room and screeched dad's name, "*Rocky!*" so loud, she frightened me. Spit was flying out of her mouth as she was screaming and crying. She was scaring me because I still didn't comprehend at that point, that my dad had left us, and that it was him that took all of our stuff.

From that moment, life was different.

No, We Weren't Wanted by the FBI

Mom quit school after finishing ninth grade so she could help support grandma and her three brothers. Because of her lack of education, she never had a decent paying job. So, we lived with friends or relatives who had room to take us in, or we had to live in low-income housing.

Mom and I moved quite often. You would have thought she was wanted by the FBI or in the military. But, I think she was just searching for something better for us. By the time I graduated from high school, we had moved twenty-two times, between four different states, and I attended 12 different schools. I remember changing schools three times in the third grade alone. Consequently, I quickly grew accustomed to leaving friends behind and starting over.

Napoleon Hill said, "*It takes half your life before you discover life is a do-it-yourself project.*" I think I figured that out long before half my life played out. I realized early on that I was responsible for creating my reality. I had to learn to bond with people fast and to fit in because the new kid in school always became a target. So, I quickly learned how to build rapport and as a result, kids liked me. I never became a target. I sincerely believe all the moving and changing schools helped me become the amiable, and likeable man I am today.

By the time I graduated from high school, I was a master at building rapport and fitting in. I could easily connect with people from ages five to seventy-five. It became second nature to me, and that skill served me well in business later in my life.

The Entrepreneurial Bug

Growing up in a low-income family wasn't a real issue for me. I didn't really know we were on the lower end of the income spectrum. We could either afford to buy something or we couldn't; I never labeled us as being poor. But, until I got older it didn't occur to me that I didn't have to settle for just getting by, and that there were other ways to make money besides employment.

I wasn't born with an entrepreneurial spirit, but that changed in the fall of 1987. I remember the very moment my entrepreneurial juices started flowing. I was lying in bed late night channel surfing, and I stumbled across an infomercial for a 'no-money-down' real-estate seminar.

No money required? How could that be?

There, on my twenty-five inch RCA television, was a Vietnamese man with a funny accent telling me how I could invest in real estate without putting any money up front. He was going to teach me the same strategies he used to become a wealthy real-estate investor, and his free seminar was coming to Las Vegas.

I was intrigued, and I was excited!

I started dreaming for the first time in my life. The possibility of creating an income stream outside of my job was exhilarating. I was so excited that my fingers were shaking while I was dialing the toll-free number. I don't remember the conversation I had with the operator; but by the end of the phone call, I was registered for the upcoming seminar.

I purchased the no-money-down real-estate course at the free seminar, took it home and devoured the information. I wish I could tell you a rags-to-riches story from there, but that wasn't the case. I did make two appointments with property owners, but I was told, "*No, not interested*," both times. So, I got discouraged and gave up.

I almost laugh at myself now, looking back. There were so many things I could have done differently if I had the knowledge and wisdom then, that I have now. But, at that point in my life, I wasn't familiar with Napoleon Hill or his book *Think and Grow Rich* (TGR). I was a kid who was raised mostly on welfare and food stamps and I didn't know the first thing about Definiteness of Purpose, Applied Faith, or Self-Discipline. In fact, I had never heard of or learned any of his seventeen principles.

My first exposure to TGR and Napoleon Hill's 17 principals was in the early 90's. I had joined my first network marketing company selling financial products, and that company promoted TGR to all of the associates. They promised we would be successful if we mastered the seventeen principals in the book. I consumed every word and believed one hundred percent in all of the principles. The book became my bible for success.

I learned that success was only dependent on my thought processes, which was a new concept for me. Before that, I thought that people were just lucky, or they were born positive, determined, focused, confident, and successful.

Because I had Faith, chapter three of TGR, and believed what my managers told me, I created remarkable results with that company. I became one of the top recruiters locally for the company because of my consistent actions (TGR - chapter 9, persistence).

I learned how to prospect for leads/recruits in the mall, grocery stores, or wherever I happened to be. Part of my daily method of operation was to talk to a minimum of ten people per day, five days per week. The motivation to reach my goals was driven by definiteness of purpose, faith, and organized planning, amongst other principles in the book.

The month I became the number one recruiter and was promoted to RVP (Regional Vice President) happened because of my consistent action and unwavering belief. The month prior to my promotion I prospected well over 300 people and solicited 247 names and phone numbers for leads. My consistent efforts, plus that final push, resulted in my sponsoring 17 new recruits and my team producing enough sales volume to earn my RVP promotion.

Obviously, my results were quite different from my no-money-down real-estate adventure. The results were better because I was better. I was better because my thoughts and my belief system were different. And my thoughts and belief system were different because I read *Think and Grow Rich* and implemented the principles outlined in the book.

> *"First comes thought; then organization of that thought, into ideas and plans; then transformation of those plans into reality. The beginning, as you will observe, is in your imagination."*
>
> — Napoleon Hill

Ready, Fire, Aim

"You're crazy!" I said to Daryn emphatically. *"That's a huge undertaking. Besides that, we don't have any experience."* I added smugly. As those last few words were leaving my lips I reflected on what I learned from *Think and Grow Rich* years earlier: Desire – the starting point of all achievement, Faith – the second step towards riches, Auto-suggestion – influencing the subconscious mind. All of the principles came flooding into my mind like a torrent of knowledge from a ruptured dam. "We could do this," I thought to myself excitedly. Of course, I didn't let Daryn know what I was thinking. I had just snapped at him like he was crazy and I had to save face. I told him I would think about it and the

next day I told him I was in.

Three days after I accepted Daryn's offer, we met and discussed the details of the enormous project with a group of five others that Daryn had shared his dream with. By the end of the six-hour meeting I was tasked with the marketing and advertising for the project. I didn't know very much about marketing or advertising, but I was willing to take on the role. "*Ready, fire, aim!*" as they say.

I took my role seriously. I devoured everything I could find on marketing (TGR - chapter 5, specialized knowledge). I started with a used marketing textbook from the local university, that I borrowed from a friend. I learned some basics, but the book was boring and I was getting frustrated and discouraged, so I turned to Amazon. It was a fairly new website back then, which still sold books exclusively. I did a search for marketing books and I was elated to find so many to choose from. The very first book I ordered was *Guerrilla Marketing* by Jay Conrad Levinson. I received the book within the week and finished it in two days.

I was hooked!

I went back to Amazon and ordered *Guerrilla Marketing Excellence, Guerrilla Advertising, Guerilla Marketing Attack*, and *Guerrilla Marketing With Technology*. I didn't realize it at the time, but I was preparing myself to become an expert and possess specialized knowledge that would eventually serve many people. Marketing and advertising became my new obsession. I read books by Seth Godin, Al Reis, Robert Chialdini, Jack Trout, Joe Pulizzi, Edward Bernays, Leo Burnet, and Jay Abraham, to name a few. I spent thousands of dollars on books and courses that year and became a walking encyclopedia of marketing and advertising.

Unfortunately, no one else on the team read *Think and Grow Rich*. Our friends, who committed to the project, just gave up. They weren't willing to educate themselves, develop a definiteness of purpose, or have unwavering faith in what we were doing. So Daryn's big project fell apart after a few months. But that wasn't the end for me. Marketing and advertising were in my blood now. I was ready to write the next chapter of my life.

I was excited to share my knowledge, so the first thing I decided to do was teach a marketing class at the local college. One of the weakest skill sets small business owners have is marketing and advertising, so I knew my knowledge base would be greater than anyone that would attend my class. And I knew I could help them save money and spend money more wisely for their marketing and advertising efforts. I had no experience teaching, especially at a college. But I had a definiteness of purpose and I was armed with the other principles of TGR.

I ended up teaching 2 adult education classes at the College of Southern Nevada. The first course to get approved by the college was a twelve-week course called *"Power Marketing Concepts for Small Business Owners."* The second was a short four-hour course called *"Schmoozing in the New Millennium"* which, educated small and home-based business owners on how to network themselves and their business effectively.

To say I was nervous the first day of class is an understatement. I had sweat rings on my shirt before anyone even arrived and I was sick to my stomach. I wanted to throw up in the trashcan and go home.

What was I doing? What do I know? Will they like me? They paid for this class with their hard-earned money; do I have anything of value to offer these people? All of these thoughts were racing through my head, as I stood alone in front of the classroom. The overhead projector was glaringly bright, broadcasting my first transparency on the screen – Welcome to Power Marketing Concepts.

I felt like a fraud.

Then I remembered two quotes. One by Nelson Mandela, *"I learned that courage was not the absence of fear, but the triumph over it. The brave man is not he who does not feel afraid, but he who conquers that fear."* And the other by Napoleon Hill, *"Fear is nothing more than a state of mind."* At that point, I felt more empowered. I did some deep breathing, cleared my mind, and kept repeating to myself, *"This is not about me, it's about them. How can I best serve them?"* Over and over again. Deep breathing, *"This is not about me, it's about them. How can I best serve them?"*

By the time the first student walked into class I had stopped sweating and I wasn't nauseas anymore. I was actually excited. I was ready to rock-this-thing!

I got into-the-zone that night. I felt like I was walking in the clouds. All the students stayed awake, practically on the edge of their seats for most of the class. Everyone was participating, eagerly asking questions, explaining their situations and looking for solutions.

Nearly every student that night, came up to thank me when the first class was over. At least half of the class shared their excitement for the next eleven weeks. I was so emotional by the time they all left that I almost broke down and cried. Well, if I am going to be honest, I shed a few tears. I, me, Scott Venezia had something of value to offer and the students were appreciative of what I had taught them and hungry for more. I was helping affect change in their business practices.

After the success of the class and receiving positive feedback from the students, I decided the next step was to create my own seminars. I was getting paid twenty-one dollars an hour to teach at the college, but I could charge more, spend less time and still give a ton of value by doing my own seminars. I already had all the material from the college courses I was teaching, so why not get paid a lot more, for delivering the same content.

I started going to more networking events and connecting with hundreds of small business owners. I was really surprised that so many people wanted what I had to offer, because I was taking my knowledge for granted. But. I quickly realized how valuable it was.

By the time things were in full swing I was doing a four-hour workshop named Schmoozing in the New Millennium, and a full day seminar called Power Marketing Concepts. I didn't know much about running my own workshops or seminars, but I had a definiteness of purpose driving me. I figured it out as I went along. My main objective was to always deliver massive amounts of value to the participants. And it worked.

I met a lot of key people because of my networking efforts (I didn't have social media back then), and that led to other opportunities for me. Within a twelve-month period, I was teaching two classes at the college and doing my own seminars. I became a guest columnist for a national trade magazine and wrote a twelve-month series on the *Ten Commandments of Marketing*. I also became an executive board member for the American Marketing Association and was being interviewed on the local news about the classes I was teaching at the college.

All of that within a year from not knowing anything about marketing and advertising.

Now I am on to the next adventure.

My friend of twenty years, and now business partner, Rachael, wrote the following chapter in this book. She is an amazing, insightful, and powerful speaker and trainer that I am excited and privileged to work with. We are launching our coaching and seminar company later this year. We will be sharing our experiences and truths to help coaches, speakers, experts, and service based entrepreneurs. It's about teaching them how to create an extraordinary and successful business by creating loving nurturing relationships with themselves and others by Living in the Magic.

I didn't share my accomplishments to boast or brag and It wasn't meant to try and impress you, in the slightest. But, to impress upon you, the profound affects *Think and Grow Rich* had on me and my journey in life. I didn't grow up with a silver spoon in my mouth. I was just a little boy who was raised in a low income, single parent household, who moved around the country a great deal. And I wasn't taught the first thing about creating successes in my life. *Think and Grow Rich* fueled my journey and it helped me create amazing things in my life. It helped shape and mold me into the man I am today and It has changed my life permanently and forever, for the better. I will be eternally grateful to Napoleon Hill and his principles.

BIO | Scott Venezia

Scott S. D. Venezia is a professional speaker and lifestyle coach, who also has private coaching clients – other coaches, speakers and, service based entrepreneurs – that he helps to realize their greatness so they can widen their audience and affect change in more people.

Scott has one e-book to his name - *Manifesting Miracles – The Hidden Keys to Unlocking the Law of Attraction* and will soon be publishing another book called *The Art of Choice: Master the Art, Master Your Life*.

Mr. Venezia is creating a global brand and movement called *Live in the Magic*, which helps service-based entrepreneurs and professionals create successful businesses and fulfilled lives, through understanding and nurturing their relationship with themselves and with others.

If you need a dynamic and authentic speaker at your next event, or want a complimentary strategy session, you can email Scott Venezia at info@liveinthemagic.com

Website: www.liveinthemagic.com

Facebook: facebook.com/liveinthemagic

CHAPTER 6

Surviving Death Valley Helped Us Find Our Way

By: Rachael Dilling

At 10:30 in the evening the lights of our 24-hour a day city where far behind us, and the blackness of the desert landscape and appeared to wrap itself around us like a black velvet blanket. I was positive that Bryan had said to turn right at the fork; even though the walkie-talkie had been pretty garbled. David was not so sure, he and I had debated; I won, and we turned right. I soon regretted that decision. We had driven for at least 45 minutes. By the looks of it we were in the wrong place. The roads got thinner and the rocks got bigger and seemed to multiply. The only thing we saw was what the headlights revealed. This was definitely not the hot springs.

We were in the middle of Death Valley, miles from anywhere, and BAM!! The steering wheel began to shimmy, and the vehicle began to shake. I knew I had a blowout. We had hit a rock and it ripped open the side of the tire, rendering it non-repairable.

David being the hero that he is, got out, grabbed the spare from under the Acura SUV and within thirty minutes we were ready to go again. I turned over the engine, pressed the gas pedal, began to move forward, and within ten feet the shimmying came back. "*David, something is wrong.*" I said. The spare tire had imploded on the wheel and was useless.

David struggled in an attempt to fix the spare. Being October, the temperature had dropped dramatically. Gratefully I pulled on the pink and white striped ski jacket I borrowed from my daughter, Jessica. I was hungry and tired. From the back of the SUV I hollered out, "*What do you want for dinner?*" David responded, "I'm in the mood for Chinese take-out." That made me giggle, "*I'll see what I can do.*" I pulled out the lantern, the green one-burner stove, and the plastic bag of goulash I had pre-made for dinner, and poured the contents into a pot. Within moments dinner was hot and ready to eat.

The lantern kept the darkness at bay, as we sat with our feet dangling off the back of the hatchback and ate. We made the decision that the best course of action for the night was to get some sleep (it was past midnight by then) and without radio reception or cell service we really couldn't do much more. I rinsed the dishes and put them back in the big plastic camping bin. We finished emptying out the rest of the camping supplies from the back of my Acura. I pulled down the mattress that had been wrapped up with bungee cords and laid it flat, covered it with sheets and blankets, slipped into my pink Tinkerbelle night shirt and waited for David. Five minutes later he crawled into the vehicle with me, closed the hatchback, and locked the doors. It was deathly quiet and still.

As I looked out the window at the vast view of nothingness, it set the perfect scene for a horror film. I felt the fear begin to rise in me. As my chest began to tighten, I forced a deep breath and reminded myself that at this very moment I had everything I needed. I had a full tummy, a warm blanket, and my David beside me. I breathed calmly and scooted back to snuggle closer to him. "*Umm, where is the hatchet?*" I asked. He laughed and told me it was by his feet, but if it would make me feel better he would put it under his pillow. It did…and he did. We slept well.

Surviving Death Valley Helped Us Find Our Way

We had to cover our eyes as we woke because the dawn of the desert sun shone so brilliantly through the windows. It had begun to warm the land, and the stark landscape reflected the bright light. David took another look at the spare tire as I prepared breakfast. We ate our oatmeal with dried fruit and formulated a plan. First, he would walk up the large hill to the west, to see if he could get any kind of signal, anything to reach the outside world. Then we would pack what we could carry and begin our long journey back to civilization.

As he began his hike, I decided I needed to center myself. I had been an apprentice of positive thought for year and now was the time to put all the practice to work. Settled in the driver's seat which was pushed all the way back, I begin to focus on my breath...in, out, in, out. I calmed my mind, cleared my intention, declared...felt...knew it was all going to work out perfectly. We were safe. Help would find us. The tire would be repaired. It wasn't just words. For an hour I sat still, quiet, feeling assured and knowing all was going to be just fine.

> *"Perhaps we shall learn, as we pass through this age, that the 'other self' is more powerful than the physical self we see when we look into a mirror."*
>
> — Napoleon Hill, *Think and Grow Rich*

David was unable to get reception or service of any kind. From the top of the hill, he said it was desert as far as the eye could see. He figured we had gone about 20 miles off the main road and it would take around 2 days to hike out. The idea of this did not thrill me. I reminded myself to look at the positive aspects of this situation: I was here with my David who was one of the most capable men I knew, we had plenty of supplies, and I could use the exercise.

We emptied all three backpacks and filled one with two-dozen 4.5oz emergency water bags and all the lidded containers full of water we could find. The second bag was filled with food: MREs, fresh fruit, trail mix, etc. The third carried a plastic shelter; sleeping supplies, flash lights, batteries, paper goods, first aid kit, and more water. David swung the two heaviest bags onto his shoulders. One saddled his back and the other his front. He positioned the hatchet through his belt next to his Leatherman. I fitted the lightest backpack on my back along with the folding portable potty. (I'm in my 40s. I don't squat.)

I was so grateful that it was autumn and the heat was bearable. We slid our sunglasses on. I wrapped my floppy straw sun hat to my head like a bonnet, slathered myself with sunscreen and began to walk. Our pace was slow and steady. The path and the destination were clear in our minds. David was impressed at my calmness. I knew positive mental attitude was the only thing keeping me from *"freaking out."* I knew everything had to work out alright. There was no other option in my mind.

> *"Set your mind on a definite goal and observe how quickly the world stands aside to let you pass."*
>
> — Napoleon Hill, *Think and Grow Rich*

After 3 ½ miles we came to a fork in the road. This one was different from the one I had turned onto the previous night. We must have missed it in the dark. We decided to mark our path in case our friends, Kristine and Bryan, came this way looking for us. We gathered rocks and began to create a three-foot arrow. Suddenly, David stopped and fixed his gaze somewhere in the distance. He pointed over my head. *"Do you see that?"* I turned around and saw a small white moving shimmer about a half mile away. I wasn't sure if it was a mirage or an actual vehicle. My heart lifted with excitement. Maybe Kristine and Bryan had found us. Within moments we saw it wasn't their white monster truck, but a little white Dodge Charger that came into focus. What in the world was a small car like that doing on the road like this? David

Surviving Death Valley Helped Us Find Our Way

waved it down. They were lost. Apparently, they had taken the same right turn we had the night before. The woman was in a geological doctoral program in school and was looking for an historical site to do some research. She had brought her two daughters and an old family friend along for the adventure. David spoke with the friend, a retired train conductor, for several minutes about our circumstances.

The train conductor suggested we see if the Charger's spare fit the Acura. It's seemed unlikely due to the vast size difference between the two vehicles, and it was worth a try. Our new companion popped the trunk, and we unloaded our three backpacks into the available space along with my portable potty. There was only enough room in the vehicle for five people. The train conductor insisted on walking behind and said he would eventually catch up. David opened the door for me. With a bit of reluctance, I slid into the backseat. I glanced over at the two young girls. One, around 13, had bright pink hair falling across her left eye and down her back. She wore impeccable magazine-cover model make-up. It must have taken at least an hour for her to prepare that morning. In contrast her younger sister appeared as if she had just awakened from a long night of slumber: hair tussled and knotted with big brown, sleepy eyes. I introduced myself, shook their hands respectfully, and began the uncomfortable task of creating small talk. Their mother and my David conversed in the front seat as we began the trek back to our stranded vehicle.

> *"There is a difference between WISHING for a thing and being READY to receive it. No one is ready for a thing, until he believes he can acquire it. The state of mind must be BELIEF, not mere hope or wish. Open-mindedness is essential for belief."*
>
> — Napoleon Hill, *Think and Grow Rich*

"*They both have five lug nuts*", David explained to me with enthusiasm. "*It will work*". On some level I wasn't surprised, on another it did seem quite amazing. What were the odds? With ease and such grace, he changed out the spare tire on the Acura, leaving only a slight black smudge of dirt on his forehead. I reached up and smeared it some more with my thumb in an attempt to remove it. I shrugged and smiled to myself deciding to leave his face decorated as I turned back to the task at hand.

I drove the car in reverse to retrieve our train conductor. Now that the SUV was functional again, the next challenge was to turn each of the vehicles around on this narrow, one lane, rock-strewn road. We devised a strategy. Again, I drove the Charger backward, a mile up the road; this time to a wider clearing. With guidance from David I did a seven-point turn so we were facing the correct direction. Then David applied this pattern, only doing the process in four points. Show off. It took a bit more time until we were finally ready to escape from the vast raw nature of Death Valley.

We pulled into the "No-Name" gas station off the main road. David took off the spare, dropped a quarter into the water/air pump we had parked in front of, and washed the accumulated dust off of the borrowed tire. He then headed into the store to speak to the clerk.

With such gratitude, I helped our rescuers put the tire back into their trunk. I hugged both the geologist and the conductor, and gifted them with bottles of wine to say thank you. David returned at that point. "*The clerk says there is no way the Charger can make the journey to your intended destination*". I could see the disappointment in the geologist's eyes. She signed, "*Well, maybe my clan has had enough adventure for one weekend. Next time we'll have to rent a bigger car*". As they drove away, I waved and in my mind wished them well.

The clerk had also told David that the nearest tire repair store was about 2 hours away. We sat on the ledge of the cement slab in front of the store and looked at the hole where the tire

Surviving Death Valley Helped Us Find Our Way

should be. What was our next step? At that exact moment a Tough Country UTV pulled up and parked next to us. The driver stepped out dressed in old work boots, tattered jeans and a dirty white t-shirt. His beard was an inch or two long. Bearded Guy unloaded the firewood from the back of his cart and piled it by the sliding door of the convenience store. As he went about the chore at hand, we caught eyes and smiled a pleasant greeting. When he was finished he walked over and asked what happened to our tire. David explained our situation. With another kind smile he offered help: *"I have a tire repair tool in my garage. It's just a few miles up the road. I think I can fix it"*. Before I knew what was happening, David had given him the spare tire and he was gone. I thought to myself that was very trusting of David.

By now my head felt light and my stomach, woozy. I needed food. As we waited for the return of the Acura's donut, I pulled out a few MREs, tore open the pouches, added some water, and activated the heating element. In just a few moments David and I ate a nice serving of mac and cheese.

Then Bearded Guy was back. He carried the fixed spare with a sense of pride. He had been able to stretch the tire back onto the rim and fix the valve stem. David put the spare on the SUV. I offered Bearded Guy some money. He said *"no"*. I offered a few bottles of wine. He refused. *"I don't drink"*. How about MREs? He looked through our collection and chose three. He thanked us as if we had done him a favor.

With David in the driver's seat, we got back on the paved road headed home. I took his hand in mine. Touching fingers across the console, we reflected on our journey over the past 18 hours. David was amazed at how things just seemed to fall into place. The truth is, we were in a seriously dangerous situation that could have resulted in death, however, we survived not any worse for the wear.

We just followed Napoleon Hill's "principles of success", I mused. We continually used a positive mental attitude (knowing we would be okay), defined a chief aim (getting out alive), cooperation (working together with each other and our rescuers), self-discipline (walking three-and-a-half miles), more self-discipline (mentally ready to walk for two days as planned), self-confidence (never doubting that we would be alright), and initiative and leadership (developing a plan and implementing it.)

We didn't find the way to the hot springs that trip, but with preparation and positivity we survived Death Valley and found our way.

BIO | Rachael Dilling

Rachael Dilling was born and raised in Las Vegas and holds a Bachelor's degree in Workforce Education from the UNLV. She is a certified Dale Carnegie instructor, a licensed spiritual practitioner and a licensed minister.

During her career, Rachael has held various teaching posts at the College of Southern Nevada, University of Las Vegas Nevada, Dale Carnegie Training, Fred Pryor Seminars and other organizations. She ran the *"Leadership Las Vegas"* program for the Las Vegas Chamber of Commerce for two years and has worked in business development and marketing.

Rachael will use her 20+ years of experience in training and personal growth for her next project, Live in the Magic. This will help entrepreneurs and professionals create successful businesses and fulfiller lives.

For a dynamic and authentic speaker, or a complimentary strategy session to uncover the greatness locked inside you and a life of unlimited possibilities, email Rachael at info@liveinthemagic.com.

CHAPTER 7

The Fine Art of Parenting After Separation
The Power of a Positive Mental Attitude

By: Cynthia (Bester) Vos

*A joyful heart is good medicine, but a
crushed spirit dries up the bones.*

— Proverbs 17:22

How can one have a positive mindset, yet be surrounded by negative rumblings and disturbances? This is a question that all parents who have gone through a separation and then divorce seem to find themselves buried under. Some, unfortunately, never find a way to dig themselves out. It is not always as easy as simply pointing a finger at a situation or analyzing the root of dysfunction, because just as the wind changes speed and direction quickly, so can the dysfunction. And this is just the adult's emotions. Now let us put the children into the equation. This is a time when the true test presents itself and the results are often fatal. Children learn that a parent's love is not the safety they believed it to be. The family net that they knew is taken away and when a new net is not woven together swiftly, their safety plan becomes null and void.

No matter how positive the veil seems, if the bones dry up, sink or swim becomes a reality.

The following is MY story as seen through MY eyes.

I remember that it was a hot summer day and we had friends over for the weekend, full of family fun and great adventures on the lake. The ensuing couple of days after are a blur.

At the tail end of the weekend, I received some information that would forever change my future. My "*in control life*" quickly took a violent downward spin. Control of any sort was something I no longer possessed. My ability to breathe was taken away and my heart felt shattered into a million pieces.

What I do remember is my boys witnessing their strong superwoman mother collapse on the kitchen floor. I looked up and had my boys around me with fear in their eyes. At that moment, I knew I needed help. My strength had disappeared and I could not let my children come down the dark hole, I was about to enter, with me. I called one of my best friends and she quickly came to help with me with my boys and support me with finding a way to breathe. Our net had been ripped out from the bottom and until I could bring some security back into my life, I knew that there would be no security in theirs. A house of four went to a house of three. At that moment, I realized history could not be undone and there was no way to erase the scribbles of that day.

When they tell you during in-flight instructions that you need to put your oxygen mask on first, you really need to remember those instructions. Your children really do need you to put your oxygen mask on first. When mom is not breathing, children become very afraid as they watch the colour in your face fade and your body become still. You never know how you are going to react to a situation until you face it. There is no practice run. So please, put on your oxygen mask first.

After a loss, you regress to early adolescence with emotions of discontent, restlessness, doubt, despair, and longing. Then reality sets in and you realize that you are far past the point of adolescence and you begin to feel the signs of decay rather than growth.

My life was picture-perfect. There was nothing more that I could have ever asked for. Then in an instant, I found myself in a moment of crisis and caught living a life somewhere in the middle of being a story and the truth. I see now that the truth was something that I had chosen to overlook for years.

I do not want this be another sad story about a sad woman. This is not a divorce story. This is a story about a girl who comes from thick stock. A girl who has always worked hard to find a way to live a life that is true to her own unique Definiteness of Purpose through the power of a Positive Mental Attitude.

Our society is in a state of dismantling and it seems as though this is nothing new. The more research I do and the more open I am when I speak with women, the more stories I hear of others who face the challenge of maintaining their personal identity, throughout the journey of marriage, often resulting in losing access to parts of their personal tools of strength entering into the framework of motherhood not fully prepared.

In the moment of crisis, we must be able to leverage our personal principles of strength. We must be able to lead as role models with our heads high. It is our duty to ourselves and to our children. Our children cannot be dismantled. We as individuals cannot be dismantled.

Adversity Behind the Wall

I tried to dig a tunnel but the hole just got deeper and deeper and very dark and damp. Then I found that I wanted to climb out of the hole. I tried climbing the wall but it never seemed to end, so I decided it was easier to climb down again. I tried to chisel out a brick but the mortar was too strong. I was determined to find a way past this wall. I was not going to give up. I then sat with my back to the wall and cried and cried until there were no more tears. My bones and my soul ached. A small voice whispered to me - lift your head. I was so exhausted but I knew the power behind this voice. As I lifted my head I saw a line of light peeking through the wall opposite the one I had been tackling. I walked up to it and ran my hand along the wall so I could feel the light. My hand hit a latch. I quickly lifted it and a small peephole opened. It was a window I could look out. My hands shuffled around the area and I found a handle. A handle! I hesitated and looked back at the wall that had defeated me. Had I tried everything I could? Had I given up too soon? The voice then said - turn the handle and open the door. I opened the door and saw the most beautiful field. I stepped into that field and felt my true self-coming alive. All along, that door was there for me to open. I just had to turn around and not be afraid.

— Cynthia Vos

Rachel Cusk sums it up best when she says, "*As it stands, motherhood is a sort of wilderness through which each woman hacks her way, part martyr, part pioneer; a turn of events from which some women derive feelings of heroism, while others experience a sense of exile from the world they knew.*"

I was very fortunate as a young adult to have been educated in the Napoleon Hill's Success Principles and that is where I needed to return catching my breath and relearning how to breathe into MY oxygen mask.

Definiteness of Purpose is the starting point of all achievement.

For me, there is nothing that compares to the moment when I found out that I was going to become a mother. As soon as I found out I was pregnant, I jumped into wanting to be a parent. Like most things I am faced, I entered with full force.

I have been fortunate to have accomplished many goals I have set out in my life. I started university at 17 and graduated with distinction. I was the youngest to ever be accepted into the Masters program at my university. I was the only one who wrote a thesis in my graduating class. I was the first person, a woman, to win Young Entrepreneur of the Year through the Chamber of Commerce. I become the first second-generation owner of a We Care franchise in Canada. I lived in my dream house. I owned my dream car. I worked hard. I played hard. And I was a good mom. I had a marriage that everyone thought would last forever. People would continually tell me how they envied my life. I had every reason to live with a positive mental attitude. My world was a masterpiece. And I controlled my destiny.

Then I was faced with the emanate question…how had I suddenly hit this wall of adversity?

My first lesson in this journey was that I needed to learn how to tell my story - not list my resume. Life is so rich with warm memories, whether they are happy or sad and this is the direction my thoughts had to travel. My accomplishments were great. But my memories were greater. My children and their growth were my main purposes in life.

I quickly learned that there is no blueprint for **after** "*having it all*".

There are no guidebooks and your entire life becomes a transcript that is open for interpretation and becomes a topic widely discussed among many. My status as a wife and woman had suddenly changed drastically. When I was able to look past myself, I was able to find a blueprint that had the ability to become a stable foundation for our newly formed family dynamic. The blueprint of being a mother remained, my other roles may have shifted, but being a mother remained constant. My children needed me to continue to be the mother that they had grown with. Just as importantly, they also needed their father. As those who know, this is the portion of the battle where there must be a way to find a truce. Divorce may have a clear 50/50 split of possessions, but we have to remember that children do not exactly operate well when cut in half.

> *"Any definite purpose that is deliberately fixed in the mind and held there, with the determination to realize it, finally saturated the entire subconscious mind until it automatically influences the physical action of the body toward the attainment of that purpose."*
>
> — Napoleon Hill

Children feel your vibration. This is a huge responsibility to hold, as the future of your children is controlled by the power of your thoughts and your leadership. It took me some time to realize that I needed to look ahead and visualize my own possible growth in a direction that was now my full responsibility. I had to take personal responsibility for my actions; all of my actions, especially those that affected my parenting. Part of defining my definite purpose was to write out a clear and concise statement of MY goals. I had lived in a world for years thinking of life goals as OUR goals so this change in direction was extremely challenging. I began with writing a letter to myself and titled it *"Who Is Cyndi?"* At first, I kept this letter to myself as I needed to regain my own mental well-being. I did not want any outside influences involved as everyone else held an opinion and emotions, which were not in my control, and not always in my best interest. At a time when I was trying to regain control of myself, it was extremely important to focus on my own mental attitude and keep it safe.

This activity helped me rethink my values on self-reliance, personal initiative, imagination, renewed my enthusiasm, self-discipline and concentration of effort. It also helped me focus on one my specializations – being a woman and the gift of motherhood. It after all, was one of my major fields of interest.

This letter also alerted my mind to new and exciting opportunities and it gave me courage to follow through with action. This letter started to put me into action and lead me to re-establish my lines of integrity. Life cannot be managed by crisis. A strong sense of confidence in your own veracity and character is what leads us through this journey.

This letter also slowly prepared my mind for faith, something that had been lost. I found myself longing for faith. I felt it as a child, but it started to fade away as a teenager and became a myth as a young adult. It always seemed as though it was around the next corner of my journey. I knew I had it. I knew it had me. I just had to trust faith. I knew that in order for my bones to stay intact, I needed faith along with a positive mind to give me freedom from fear, doubt, discouragement, indecision and procrastination.

The most important relationship is the one you have with yourself. You'll find almost no one will treat you better than you treat yourself, and if they do, they likely have an ulterior motive. The most important person to fall in love with is yourself. Your love and respect you have for yourself will motivate and inspire you to teach your children how to treat you correctly and they will learn how to treat themselves and others in the world according to the model you exhibit. It works with all relationships.

I became responsible for my own happiness.

These are some questions that I asked myself.

- Why am I here?
- What is the top purpose of my life?
- What are the most important things I want to accomplish in my life?
- What fulfills me above all other things?
- What would you do if you had a million dollars in the bank?
- In what ways would your life change?
- What would you do differently?
- What three goals do you want to accomplish in each decade of your life?
- What are the three things that you would regret not doing if you were informed you were about to die?
- What is the one thing that you would want to define your professional career when you die?
- What is the one thing that you would want to define your personal growth when you die?

I had to simplify my life. I had to answer these questions and put together a simple statement that I could read to myself whenever I felt that I was wavering. This is what I put together. This is the blueprint I wanted for my life.

I am a woman who continues to grow in character and spiritual maturity.
I share the feminine wisdom I have gained to encourage others to reach their full potential.
I respectfully acknowledge that I am a woman who has embraced passion and entrepreneurial traits for the good of her family and community.
I have a partner to stand by and support, recognizing and appreciating that he is also standing by me.

*I am a woman of great worth in the eyes of my partner, entrusting in his leadership for our future.
We strengthen each other through patience, kindness and love.*

From an early age, I knew that my essence has never been one of simplicity. There was always a fine balance between grace and a lost soul, as I too, was a child of divorce. I was all too familiar with the consequence of imbalance in harmony.

Mastermind Alliance

When I imagine myself as an old woman at the end of my life and ask myself how I will evaluate my time here, there is only one questions that concerns me: Did I love well? The Invitation, Oriah

"The Mastermind Alliance principle consists of an alliance of two or more minds working together in perfect harmony for the attainment of a definite objective. It is referred to as the very hub or axis of the entire philosophy."

— Napoleon Hill

When your marriage falls apart, your entire foundation is ripped from underneath you. In the end, there is really no way to go back and fix anything between the relationship of wife and husband. Taking the time to remap your relationship is essential for your mental health as well as your parenting partner and your children. This is not a win lose competition. As an alliance, you must continue to look in the same direction regarding the children.

Precedent. Remember how I said that a positive mind is held when you do not let others creep into your subconscious? Everyone wanted me to follow precedent. The first lawyer I met had a take down attitude like no one I had ever encountered. This is when I realized that I had to revisit the shape of my mastermind alliance with my children's father. I was not going to wound my children more than they had been.

They say that the natural instinct of a mother is the *"they belong to me"* stance. What is often overlooked is that children belong to the father as much as they belong to the mother. I know this is a very controversial statement and emotions shoot off in all sorts of directions. The mother in me wants so much to hold on to the "ownership" and the child in me so wants a relationship with both my mother and father. What we need to realize is that we are not being denied the full scope of motherhood after separation. Nothing is taken from us. We still get to watch our children at concerts, birthdays, graduations, weddings, funerals, etc. The reality is that I would still experience these events as their mother, just not as their father's wife.

Perfect harmony something that may seem impossible to envision. However, you must keep any thoughts of discord out of your alliance. I think about the harmonic difference between the music of Beethoven and Bartok or the melodies expressed in country music and aggressive heavy metal riffs. At the end of the day all music is formulated around a seven-note scale. Harmony is not going to occur quickly after a divorce. What once was whole is now separate.

This new form of harmony must be cultivated and given time to grow using these four elements: confidence, understanding, fairness and justice.

Confidence is built on proven fidelity from positive contributions of both partners. Faithfulness of parenting becomes the focus and loyal observance of obligation for that role needs to be maintained. Understanding. Each parent must possess complete knowledge and comprehension of the nature, significance, and implication of the situation. Fairness. Everyone must agree at the outset on their contribution. A parenting agreement prevents dissension. Justice. Deal with each other on the highest ethical level and create an environment that encourages no one member to seek an unfair advantage.

First you must learn how to form an alliance with yourself in a positive frame of mind. As I have stated numerous times, as this is a lesson that takes a longer time to learn, I am responsible for my own happiness. You must first condition your mind to believe in whatever you are asking the members of your alliance to do for you. You cannot operate a mastermind with a negative mind. You must stay away from your group until you yourself are positive. Your mental attitude determines your success or failure.

> *"Success attracts more success while failure attracts more failure."*
> — Napoleon Hill

So how do you form a healthy relationship with a partner who has put you in a place where you need an oxygen mask? You dig deep and reflect on the 12 riches of life: positive mental attitude, sound physical health, harmony in human relationships, freedom from fear, the hope of achievement, the capacity for faith, willingness to share one's blessings, a labor of love, an open mind on all subjects, self-discipline, the capacity to understand people and financial security. You do this all as parenting partners.

The hardest part of this is that there cannot be a counseling or coaching agenda. Both parties must acknowledge that a personal agenda must not enter into this relationship and there must be no negative gossip. Yes, it did take time to get to this point. And yes, I think I did bang my head against the wall a couple of times.

A mastermind will enable you to overcome any obstacle that may stand in the way of your major purpose. In this case, raising healthy children who are loved by both parents. Active, perfect harmony, courage, faith and common goals are the objective.

In order for this to work, we must learn how to communicate often, seamlessly, outside of meetings, authentically, honestly, and compassionately. Collaborate by listening, encouraging, opening up, and remembering having fun. I do realize that this may be pushing a lot of boundaries and that the comfort zone may take months or even years to achieve, but the end goal is still the same as when you were married.

Children are very attuned to thought messages. We as adults need to be careful of the thoughts we transmit and the ones you pick up and allow to remain in your consciousness.

As the adults in this safety net, we must give clear unmistakable signals to our crew. We cannot equate cooperation with a mastermind. A mastermind gives you full access to everyone's spiritual power. The minute there is a dominant there is a problem. Back up and regroup.

I was fortunate in that my parenting partner was also familiar with Napoleon Hill's Success Principles. He understands their importance and how they can help us lead healthy successful lives. Both of my boys participated in a Success Principles weekend when they turned eight years old. They both understand the role of a mastermind alliance, which helps us parents with an integrity check now and then.

Oxygen mask is secure.

The Fine Art of Parenting After Separation

BIO | Cynthia (Bester) Vos

Cynthia (Bester) Vos holds a Bachelor of Music, Master of Education and a Post Graduate Certification in Executive and Personal Coaching. She is currently completing her Leadership Certification through the Napoleon Hill Foundation. Her professional business career began under the direction of her entrepreneurial parents who were followers of the Success Principles. Cynthia focused in healthcare with the company We Care Health Services, specializing in palliative care, for 20 years, serving as the CEO for 10 years. She sold the company when she was 39 and soon to follow the opportunity came to head the final company under the family umbrella. Cynthia takes pride in having the opportunity to carry the legacy forward. She now runs that company with her (soon to be) husband Dave. She has had the opportunity to perform as a solo concert pianist in Canada, England, Poland, Russia, Belarus, Ukraine and the United States. Cynthia is also very active in the fitness community and competes nationally.

Cyndi (Bester) Vos

She can be contacted at cyndibester@gmail.com or follow her at Cyndi Bester on Facebook. You will find her soon on www.fashionablemind.com.

CHAPTER 8

GRATITUDE FOR VICTORIOUS LIVING

By: Christy Onabu

Positive Mental Attitude (PMA) is attitude of the highest order. PMA begins with the admonition; *"Keep your mind on the things you want"*.

Keep your mind on the things you want and off the things you don't want. Growing up was tough, yet very interesting. I desired more than anything else in life but happiness, and understood that this one thing I desired most is totally dependent on my thoughts, the way I think. Thoughts generate attitude and attitude in return, influences thought. This cycle is one thing every man passes through and the outcome is either negative or positive, depending on one's mental attitude. I realized that we all have a dual personality: one is positive and has a great capacity for belief; the other is negative and has an equally great capacity for unbelief. I was determined to place myself on the side of the personality that believes and get the unbelief personality disappear by not exercising it. I wanted the world I live in to fit my own chosen positive pattern, which I began by adopting Passive Resistance. I refused to accept from life, or anyone else, anything that I do not desire. I remember always the story of the hero who brought independence to India, Mahatma Gandhi, who proved this simple method of Passive Resistance to be more powerful than the great British military forces.

Life is all about choices and PMA is making the right choices.

Every man at birth was handed two envelops by Infinite Intelligence (Napoleon Hill). The first envelop contained REWARDS and the other contained PENALTITIES. Those who neglect to take possession of their minds and direct them toward desirable objectives will get the penalties; which are:

- A life of poverty and misery.
- Mental and physical ailments of many kinds.
- Self-limitations that bind you to mediocrity.
- Fear in all its destructive forms.
- Dislike of your occupation.
- Many enemies and few friends.
- Every type of worry known to humanity.
- Being a victim of every negative influence you encounter.
- Subjection to the influence and control of other people.
- A wasted life that gives nothing to the betterment of humanity.

I desired the rewards for those who take possession of their minds and direct them toward desirable objectives; which are:

- A Positive Mental Attitude.
- The privilege of placing yourself on the path to success.
- Attracting only the circumstances that make for success.
- Sound health.
- Financial independence.
- A labor of love of your choosing.
- Peace of mind.
- Applied Faith that makes fear impossible.
- Enduring and meaningful friendships.
- Longevity and a well-balanced life.
- Immunity against all forms of self-limitation.
- The wisdom to understand yourself and others.

PMA is the only condition of mind that permits you to get on the path to success and stay there.

I wanted an exceptionally exciting life – family, work, and friends. I had this inner confusion, which also showed up on the outside. I thought deeply to be different; I desired life without fear of people and compromise, yet with the highest reference to God and His creation. I heard His still small voice speaking to me all the time, *"Dare to be different, dare to work hard and smart and dare to educate yourself on life success skills."*

There were very strong negative influences around me, from peers at every stage of my life, lower grade, higher grade, work and family. They still exist but who cares. Every thought of living a negative life and engaging in any life demeaning actions never went down well with me. I was almost caught a few times and had no peace, had sleepless nights even when no one knew what I had done. I was emotionally devastated so many times in my life and got no help. The positive influence from my father got its place in my subconscious mind without a single knowledge of what that meant, how powerful it was and will turn out to be even at this moment.

Indeed, God has abundance of grace for those who desire good things of life and a better way to live.

A victorious life to me is simply a life with a conscience void of offence to God and Man. It is to wake up, go about my business and return home to sleep and wake the next day without an iota of doubt that I have treated everyone that I came across fairly and justly.

It is to forgive others and have others forgive me when I have done them wrong. Forgiveness allows for the mind to be freed up and you can then concentrate on your **Definite Major Purpose.**

I sought for that personality, that mindset, that quality, and Infinite Intelligence (God) provided the platform. **The key tenets of PMA philosophy** is *"what the mind can conceive and believe, it can* *achieve.*" I needed to create this personal reality through a positive belief system. I needed training, a platform to keep my mind on the good things of life. I wanted my Definite Major Purpose clearly defined, take personal initiative and achieve.

My elder sister recommended *"Think and Grow Rich"* in 2003 with books written by other great achievers, and that was the vehicle I needed to run with my vision. This was the beginning of my journey to a happier, healthier and wealthier living. Ever since I read *"Think and Grow Rich"* the first time, I have not stopped studying, practicing and teaching the *17 Principles of Success* by Napoleon Hill, who taught that the universal laws allow us to focus our mind on whatever we desire. It also allows us to create our own plan for attaining our desire. The law also repays our efforts with those good things of life mentioned in the first sealed envelope labeled "REWARDS."

PMA Is Going The Extra Mile

PMA is to live a life of service to God and humanity without the feeling of being burdened. I remember some very important life transforming events as a child between ages 9 - 12 years.

I opted to trade, and had my piggy bank to assist my father feed his large nuclear and extended family. It was my choice borne out of deep compassion and love for him. I have seen that single act paid off, even as I am still alive and work as though it's for my entire father's family; by assisting financially, spiritually and emotionally to family members without feeling the burden. It can only be through this simple awesome unequalled quality and philosophy – PMA. The Scriptures from the Holy Bible thought us the greatest lesson on Giving – "*It Is More Blessed To Give Than To Receive.*"

I recall sitting in the Saint John The Baptist Catholic Church, Agbani, Enugu State, in eastern Nigeria with other children between the ages of 8-12yrs. It was a spiritual training class to qualify us for water baptism, confirmation and Holy Communion in the Catholic Church. This particular day the priest sent for the Catechist who was giving us some instructions. The man stood up to go, scratched his head and asked who amongst us would hold brief for him. We were dumbfounded, totally confused and disconnected. None of the children expected this offer or had any idea how to go about it.

Suddenly I heard a still small voice say

> *"Christy take it up, yes you can, you have watched him read the catechism book, and asked the children to repeat them after him and as well as recite them. Go ahead."*

I stretched my hand and collected the booklet and with a low voice said to him, *"Sir, I will hold brief until you return."* I was eleven years plus and I held brief and by the time the catechist returned to the class, he couldn't believe what he noticed but allowed me carry on until the end of the class. My peers were comfortable and connected so easily with me. I was patient with them and they felt more relaxed. I was all smiles and took them through the readings and recitations such that it was easier for them to learn and memorize so quickly. We got through the baptism and confirmation class that year and that marked the beginning of my teaching career.

In 1982, just after my high school exams and waiting for admission into the University, I volunteered to serve my community as a teacher at the community high school and was later employed by the state government as an auxiliary teacher. This I did for a period of about six months and then proceeded to the university. I paid my first year tuition and had enough to feed from my savings, as I was still in a Master Mind Alliance with my father in the spirit of harmony. My Dad was a vibrant and compassionate community leader highly respected for his positive contributions and leadership.

Altruism pays. I was young and now am growing older, yet am never tired of doing more than what I am paid for. Living and performing averagely is not PMA. PMA to me is to get out of my comfort zone and think outside the box. Ordinary people can live and do extraordinary things making our world a better place. I have my quota to contribute, no matter the magnitude, I am glad I have risen up to that. I have worked with groups and organizations to raise funds and materials of different kinds to support the less privileged individuals of different ages, families, churches, schools and communities and put smiles and hope in their lives. The tested and proven Law of Compensation is ever at work in my live and family and I am privileged.

PMA is the foundation on which all prayers are expressed through Applied Faith.

Prayer is often thought of as a way to get something for oneself from Infinite Intelligence and viewed as a way to focus your mind on your **Definite Major Purpose.**

My Dad, by his own way of life thought me that all things are possible. Not one day did I hear my father talk negatively despite the great challenges and adversity he had having to carter for his many children and wives. I think he took responsibility for all his actions and was determined to face the outcome positively. Till this moment I believe strongly that it is weakness and lack of a Positive Mental Attitude for parents not to provide the true leadership required in their homes with small sized nuclear families in this 21st century. Down from the 1980s, we've seen, learned, read and heard stories of fathers and mothers who worked hard; had absolute control over their thoughts, controlled their emotions and actions and raised up their children. I am a beneficiary. After my Dad's death in 1993, I was faced with the challenge of finding another life mentor or role model whose thoughts, words and actions depicted possibility for what others felt was impossible.

Inside of me, I could sense and feel strongly that I occupy an important position in my family and my workplace. I could feel or sense the two envelops handed over to me at birth containing lists of rewards and penalties. I needed to take possession of my mind and use it to achieve my goals and enjoy the rewards. The still small voice within tells me that I was on the path of success. I needed to choose success as my destination and ride on to victory. Nature abhors vacuum (emptiness) and idleness (lack of action).

A positive mind finds a way something can be done; a negative mind looks for all the ways it can't be done. People all around me spoke about life being a struggle. I had a job and a good one comparable to peers and friends. Inside, I saw opportunities; outside was problems and struggles. I was on a journey (searching for a way to remain positive and focused on what my mind was seeing - success, helping people become better, creating multiple streams of income (MSI), meeting people around the world, travelling with family and having fun. **Success attracts more success while failure attracts more failure**.

I understand from trainings and the study of Napoleon Hill philosophy that the universal law has determined that I shall move in the direction of my dominant thought. If I put my mind to work with a positive mental attitude; and I believe in success as my entitlement, my belief will guide me toward whatever success I want. I was and I am still determined to enjoy the rewards of taking possession of my mind and direct them towards desirable objectives. I have to stay above board to overcome the cultural bias towards negative thinking and problems. I formed **Mastermind Alliance** with people who are truly free, who have established the proper system for controlling and directing their own thoughts. I needed those who surpassed me as my pacemakers. I had firm determination not only to catch up with them, but bypass them. Prayer is key in my life. I do not just confess my faith in the Infinite Intelligence; I apply my faith and receive positive outcomes.

I have learned the power of gratitude in every situation.

Express gratitude daily for being given the right to completely control your mind. Ask for guidance so that you may use this profound gift wisely in all your thoughts and acts.

Express gratitude for the influence that caused you to improve your Mental Attitude.

Believing where belief is justified:

- Existence of Infinite Intelligence. (God) – I believe and I live my beliefs.
- Ability to become free and self-determining as your greatest gift from your Creator – Peace of Mind is the Creators greatest gift to me and my family.

Create a grateful heart. Maintain a grateful heart. Overcoming every problem begins with a grateful heart.

Thanks to all the prayer teams I have partnered with, my role models and mentors all over the world; my Dad of blessed memory Thomas Honeycomb Okochi, Florence my elder sister, my entire family, my husband Emmanuel, you let me be the Courageous and Amazing Christy I am today. Great Teachers from the Napoleon Hill Foundation, Tom Cunningham, you got me into writing, my dream of many years back now being accomplished. Jeremy Razor for encouraging me to contribute a chapter in our first book "*Refusing To Quit*", The Napoleon Hill French Lick Indiana Class of March 2015, you sparked the fire that is burning and refining up till this moment. All my life teachers and all those whose lives, books, tapes, stories, dreams and inspirations has made me stay "PMA" all the way. I am forever grateful to all of you. Be assured that I am a true ambassador of this all-important 7th principle of one of the Greatest Wise Man that ever lived on this planet earth Napoleon Hill. Thank you, thank you, thank you.

I pray that God our Creator will find us all with hands lifted up in thanksgiving for all His blessings.

Remember that to achieve anything worthwhile in life, you must apply PMA. Positive Mental Attitude essential to your well-being and success.

If the man is right, his world will be right. PMA ALL THE WAY!

Christy Onabu

Nigeria.

BIO | Christy Onabu

Christy Onabu is one of the foremost Nigerian ambassador and crusader of *Think and Grow Rich* and the Napoleon Hill's *17 Success Principles*. A coach, mentor and change advocator.

Manager Supply & Distribution with the Nigerian National Petroleum Corporation and Founder of Thomas Honeycomb Foundation, an NGO that is engaged in empowering individuals and groups to find a better way to live and have their dreams accomplished. Initiator, *"The Change Advocates"* (a mind school) aimed at helping citizens in her country Nigeria to develop Positive Mental Attitude (PMA) with focus on Napoleon Hill's principles she considers key to their success. She discovered Napoleon Hill's *Think and Grow Rich* in 2003 and is currently NHF Certified Leader working on her *"Project PMA Nigeria"*, documenting feedback from over 600 free copies of *"Think and Grow Rich"* given out. She holds a Masters Degree in Biochemistry.

For more information contact her via email at thcwisdom@yahoo.co.uk

Facebook: ProjectPMANigeria

CHAPTER 9

Staying Positive In a Hectic Negative World
By: Peter Kamerman

"Nothing great was ever achieved without a positive mental attitude."

— Napoleon Hill

Why is there so much negativity?

It really is no surprise that it takes a lot of focus and work to stay positive in this fast paced hectic world we live in. It seems we have to work harder at everything and we are expected to settle for less while the cost of living sours out of control. Then we go and drown our negative thoughts by watching TV shows and movies that seem to thrive on violence and negative or by spending hours submersed in social media. More and more families are spending their evenings with each member of the family in a different room on a different device. Children today are connected to technology though a digital intravenous tube or umbilical cord feeding their brains with endless negative information. Communication is predominately done through text messaging and rarely is a phone call made. This eliminates the emotional aspects or meaning other than what is expressed through emojis, which can often lead to misinterpretation. Every action is caught on video and streaming through social media within minutes, often throwing lives into instant turmoil. Our PMA is in serious trouble!!

My wife and I have 4 children ranging from age 4 to age 17. We allow very limited access to technology and especially social media. Not one of our children has a smart phone or a Facebook account. It is becoming very difficult to keep them away but I know they are better off going without as long as possible.

Why doesn't everyone strive for ultimate happiness?

As Earl Nightingale talks about in his classic *The Strangest Secret*, most people simply do not think. They conform to what the 95% of society does without taking time to really evaluate their own potential. It seems to be the easy way out. That's all they know so that's what they do because that's what their parents did and that's what their friends do. It's safe!! Most people don't really know exactly what they want out of life. They will say they want more money, they want a bigger house, and they want a financial nest egg. That's usually as far as it goes for many. They want these things but they don't do the actions required to achieve them. They don't write down their goals because they don't have any. Isn't that sad?

A little about myself and what brought me here.

I always believed there was more to life than working a 9 to 5 job. I started reading personal development books when I was 17 and was very entrepreneurial. I realized that I could do things on my own to earn money. My parents owned a garden center and landscaping business and I remember breeding rabbits and selling the bunnies at the garden center when I was ten or eleven. In fact one of the bunnies I sold was to a young girl who years later became my wife! How's that for long term thinking? I had started planting the seeds for a positive mental attitude. To this day I am always reading books or listening to self help audios and have an extensive library of books as well as audios.

Lately I have spent a lot of time driving and listening to my audios then going to sleep with messages playing to my subconscious and as a direct result I have been experiencing some amazing success. This helps me to arrive home in great spirits as well.

Upon my arrival at home what I sometimes fail to realize is that a PMA can easily be attained when you are alone without negative distractions. As I walk through the door I often am greeting by my beautiful wife who has been running the machine in the background (I mentioned earlier our 4 children…) with all the distractions and drama that 3 girls and a boy can present. She has been getting them up and ready in the morning making sure they are clothed and fed and that all their permission slips have been signed. Then she drives them to school while often having the youngest still in tow after. Then she keeps the machine running throughout the day with laundry, shopping, baking and gardening. Then back to the school to pick up and run them to their sporting events and often coaching them as well. Of course there are the sibling feuds to break up while preparing dinner and then I arrive in good spirits while all the tension from the day comes to a boil. At this point I have no idea how her day has gone, I just realize that my positive mental attitude has just been compromised so I contribute by expressing my frustration. This of course never ends well and if you have children you can probably relate to this scenario.

The Benefits of adversity.

Just to be clear, I am writing this chapter to help myself become better just as much as I am hoping it has a few words that can also help others. I believe that every other principal and philosophy of success hinge on this very principle and until we get our Positive Mental Attitude in check we can be certain that every effort we apply to the other principles will be diluted. I say this because I spent years testing this theory and have caused many years of struggle for my family. Staying positive does not come easy to me, it requires constant work and there have been times where I simply did not have a positive bone in my body. I have been on top of the world but I have also spent a considerable time staring at the top from the bottom. During these adversities I always knew I needed to be there experiencing them and I knew there was a lesson to be learned. I would watch for the lessons and I knew when the big ones were being taught. I did not enjoy them but I knew they were necessary.

I always made an effort to get in the presence of successful people to learn from them whenever I could. I believe if you have a strong enough desire and the right attitude then you will catch the attention of successful people and they will make themselves available to you. This happened to me about ten years ago when I met a very successful entrepreneur. Her name is Marianne Noad and I was able to learn and grow so much through this business relationship. I was also given an opportunity to complete the Napoleon Hill Certification course through a gift from this incredible lady because she could see something in me that I didn't see. This was a life changing moment for me as it opened up a whole new level of thinking. I still had struggles ahead but I was armed with new ammunition. To this day she is one of my close friends and I have a tremendous gratitude toward her.

> *"Every adversity, every failure, every heartache carries with it the seed of an equal or greater benefit"*
>
> — Napoleon Hill

For me this is one of the most powerful quotes and I believe it to my core. Around 2008 to 2010 is when the economy was not very favorable to small business and my wife and I took a major hit. We lost two businesses and went through bankruptcy.

This is when your character is defined. I could have chosen to give up and conform. To say *"hey, I gave it a good effort; I guess business ownership is not for me!"* We had times where my wife was certain we would be living on the streets. I had to swallow my pride and get a construction job to keep bills paid. I always had faith that things would work out again. People would always feel bad for us because we lost our business. II would say to them *"Most of the millionaires you hear about have gone through bankruptcies at least once to get where they are, well now at least I am qualified!"*

    We lost a lot during this time but the most important things we would never loose. Nothing could take them away. We had each other and we managed to stay strong together. We had our children and they knew we were having trouble but that didn't change their love for us. We still had our freedom and most importantly we had the ability to choose to make our life great again. This last adversity was definitely the hardest one we have been through but it was also necessary. We learned incredible survival skills. We learned to respect money and how to maximize it. We learned to stay positive and believe. We learned to practice our faith. A quote I use often but have no idea of its original author is Work like it depends on you and pray like it depends on God!

> *"Don't allow adversity to steal your dream – don't even let it conceal your ultimate goal. Instead, use adversity to reveal to you the inner resources you didn't even know you possessed."*
>
> — Billy Cox

So what are some simple things we can do to keep ourselves positive?

So, there is good news and there is bad news. The good news is that while you are in a positive mental state, fear and negativity cannot also co-exist. The bad news is that while you are in a fearful or negative mental state, positive cannot co-exist.

One major contributor would be your environment. If you are in a constant negative environment you have to either change it completely or find some sort of release that allows you to find positive in it. This is crucial because your environment can either be your negative prison or your positive castle! Again, we have the ability to choose.

Just after we got married my wife and I decided to take a vacation from our home in Ontario, Canada to the West coast of British Columbia. We went with some friends for a couple of weeks to Vancouver Island and once we got back we decided that we really wanted to live there because we realized the lifestyle there was what we always dreamed of. Within 3 months we had sold our house, downsized all our belongings and were on the road to BC. We have now lived here for 17 years and I believe we live in the most beautiful place in the world. We can walk 5 minutes and be at the ocean. We can drive an hour and be on the ski hills. We have the most amazing hiking trails all around us and we have the mildest climate in all of Canada. How could anyone be negative living here? Well, there is one factor that prevents many people from living here. We get a lot of rain during the winter months. There are a lot of people that develop Seasonal Affective Disorder, also known as SAD. The symptoms can be pretty extreme – mood swings, anxiety, sleeping issues and even suicidal thoughts. It does not affect me at all but if it did, I'm certain I would chance my environment. This past winter was an interesting one. I don't think it was all that bad. It only rained two times, the first rain lasted 45 days and the second rain lasted for 35 days. That sunny day in between was sure beautiful though.

Sometimes there are people in our lives that create that negative environment and sometimes we need to make a choice to be around them less often.

> *"When you close the door of your mind to negative thoughts, the door of opportunity opens to you."*
>
> — Napoleon Hill

We have to leave the junk in the past.

We must not constantly drudge up past failures, disappointments and unpleasant circumstances. What has happened in the past does not have to define what will happen in the future. It happened and it shaped our character. That is a good thing as long as you can learn from it and leave it. We also need to forgive people who have caused us pain. It was made very clear to me when my good friend Marianne Noad told me that holding anger and resentment towards someone is very much like eating poison and expecting the other person to die. When we forgive someone it helps us release that negative and move on.

Acts of kindness.

Start saying and doing positive things to other people. Random acts of kindness like paying for someone's coffee that is in line behind you or complementing someone on their clothes or hair. In these situations both parties benefit. We feel good for making someone's day and they feel good because someone was nice to them. Sometimes there is a third winner also. Someone watching this event happen can also feel good because they witnessed someone receiving a blessing and in turn they may feel inspired to make someone else's day. It truly can be an endless ripple effect that can be created.

> *"Beginning today, treat everyone you meet as if they were going to be dead by midnight. Extend to them all the care, kindness, and understanding you can muster, and do it with no thought of any reward. Your life will never be the same again."*
>
> — Og Mandino

Keep busy all the time.

I find when I slip into the darkness most is when I have too much time on my hands. I know there are priority things I need to be doing but I end up doing very little. I decide to just play an online game first to loosen up, and then I'm going to check Facebook to make sure I'm up to date on the current events of my friends. As a result the negative feelings start creeping in. I'm pretty sure most people know what I'm talking about. The best way to keep busy is to know exactly where it is you want to go. Map out your journey in vivid details and write down these goals and dreams. Be consistent and relentless about achieving them and your time will automatically fill up.

Be accountable.

Be accountable to someone. This is also vital to staying positive. Have someone who you can be honest with and who you can share things with that will not give you the pity party but instead kick your butt and get you back in the game. A co-worker who is trying to accomplish the same goals as you but keeps running into the same roadblocks. Set up a friendly challenge and make it fun but serious. This will help both of you get results and when there are results we feel that positive attitude soar!

Don't give people permission to steal your thunder.

What I find very strange is that most people take the opinions of others so seriously. If someone speaks badly about me I really don't let it bother me... unless it's my wife (because then it is likely true). I have learned enough about the psychology of people through reading self help books to know that most people act out against others because there is some underlying issue going on in their life. Most people take it as a personal jab and starting planning out their revenge or worse, they believe those opinions.

This is another situation where we have to decide to brush it off. To just let it roll of your back because it really will have no bearing on anything if you don't allow it to. It is just a decision! If you do allow it to penetrate your beliefs then it can completely destroy your confidence and self worth. This allows uncertainty and fear to creep in and when it does then the positive is gone!

The best way to conquer this is to always love yourself and always love everyone around you.

Be the best you that you can be!

One of the most important attributes to me is that people are real. You know who they are and you trust what they say. If they say they will do something you know they will. If they tell you something you know they mean it and you know it is truth. That is who I strive to be. That is what allows me to sleep so well (and I sleep really well!).

There are so many other ways to keep a positive mental attitude that I didn't mention but these are some of the ones that I resonate with best. In this book there are many different personality types. Mine is just one. My hope is that something I shared inspires you to go out and shine your light on someone else. We need more PMA in this world so go out and do your part. It's only a decision away, and only you can decide for you.

"Recognize that your mental attitude is the one and only thing over which you, and you alone, have complete control, and exercise the privilege of taking possession of and directing your mind with a positive mental attitude."

— Napoleon Hill

BIO | Peter Kamerman

Peter Kamerman was born and raised in Ontario and always had an entrepreneurial spirit. From a young age Peter developed a strong work ethic through his family's gardening business and his experience in the construction industry. During this time he was exposed to Network Marketing and most importantly Personal Development. This new education was fascinating to Peter and his library grew quite extensively to include favorites like Napoleon Hill and Og Mandino.

At age 24 Peter was faced with a family tragedy that forced him to take over operations in the family business. This adversity was a major contributor to shaping Peter's character that would serve him throughout his life.

Peter is now in the 20th year of marriage to his amazing, beautiful wife, Christiane. Together they have 4 children. In 2000, Peter and Christiane moved their lives across Canada and relocated in Nanaimo, BC. They owned and operated several businesses within the gardening industry and in 2008 the economic downturn had caused the Kamermans to lose almost everything. Peter has always maintained faith and a Positive Mental attitude through adversities that things always have a way of working out.

Today Peter is a sales manager with Pacific Eco Tech, an eco technologies dealer for YellowBlue Canada and is enjoying amazing success. Peter attributes his attitude and determination to the success principles he learned though studying the Napoleon Hill Principles.

Peter can be reached at

Pete.kamerman@gmail.com

www.facebook.com/peter.kamerman

www.facebook.com/pacificecovanisle

www.YellowBlueCanada.ca

CHAPTER 10

If You Change Your Thinking You Change Your Reality

By: Alex Alfaro

My world has drastically changed within the past 5 years when I began my journey with *"Think and Grow Rich,"* and the Napoleon Hill Foundation, yet everything remains the same. My journey has taught me so much, but the most important thing was Napoleon Hill's *12 Riches of Life*. The first of the twelve, yet most impactful for me was a true grasp and understanding of PMA, a Positive Mental Attitude. Hill stated, *"Your mental attitude determines your success or failure,"* and that's as true a statement as you will find from any self-help book, life coach, or guru. If you change your thinking you change your reality.

1. A Positive Mental Attitude
2. Sound Health
3. Harmony in All Relationships
4. Freedom from Fear
5. The hope of Achievement
6. The Capacity for Faith
7. Willingness to Share One's Blessings
8. A Labor of Love
9. An Open Mind in All Subjects
10. Self-Discipline
11. The Capacity to Understand People

12. Financial Security

We live in a world surrounded by a sea of continuous waves of negative energy. The television is flooded with negative influences and negative subconscious programming. Movies, television shows, news and radio usually talk about, or show violence, alcohol, drug use, sex and infidelity. The networks have an obvious grasp on what fuels ratings and we are the unfortunate benefactors. It is rare to have a stranger say hello or give you a welcoming smile. You can sit next to someone for 5 hours on an airplane without one word spoken to each other. You can be enclosed within 3 feet from each other in an elevator, yet everyone has their eyes down, on their phone, or simply facing the wall. It seems like the days of receiving a friendly smile or a quick nod hello are over. Forget about having a normal conversation, everything is done via email, or by speaking in code via text. The demise of the English language is happening right before our eyes. The insidious habit of abbreviating everything in text messages has crept into the spoken word, so even when you do finally converse with someone, it can drive you crazy. Worst of all, society believes they are connected through the social media surge, yet we are completely disconnected. People spend more time comparing themselves to someone, instead of connecting with someone. They spend more time portraying someone they would like to be, instead of working towards being that person they were meant to be. This negative energy can consume you if you allow it. If you stand still and do nothing you can easily be swallowed up and dragged into the sea to drift aimlessly without purpose.

The basic problem in human life is that we suffer because we fail to distinguish between what is in our control and what is not. We are 100% in control of our thoughts, everything else about us, our body, possessions, relationships, wealth, fame, and reputation depends on factors largely outside our control. We can choose to focus on all those negative things stated above, or we can choose to focus on what is in our complete control, our thoughts. We each experience the world differently because of our thoughts and our different senses. We can each look out the same window and have a completely different picture because our vision is different, we can taste the exact same food yet have different opinions because our taste buds our different, we can listen to music and have a different emotional experience, we can walk into a garden and smell different aromas. Our personal environment, surroundings, backgrounds, friends or who we choose to surround ourselves with have given us different frames of reference. This frame of reference determines our views, beliefs, and our perception of the world. This then becomes our map, and that map becomes our territory, or our reality. The map is not the territory... we can control, and change our maps by controlling and changing one simple thing, our thoughts. There aren't two people on this earth that are experiencing the same reality, everyone's reality is different, but everyone's mental attitude doesn't need to be. We can all choose to live with PMA, a Positive Mental Attitude. Through my personal experience, the path to a positive mental attitude began with a growth mindset. My goal is to provide a few simple and easy, yet very impactful, small daily disciplines for growth that I personally practice, making sure Every Day I Live With PMA.

No Snooze

The very first commitment you make to yourself every day is to set an alarm and wake up at a certain time. The moment you hit the snooze button you have already failed on the first commitment of the day. When you fail on one commitment it makes it that much easier to fail on the rest. Don't hit snooze, when the alarm goes off, just get up. You will start the day off with discipline, and it will help you maintain the positive mental attitude needed to accomplish the tasks of the day. The best thing about this small yet effective discipline is that you are in 100% control, you are the one that chooses the time and sets the alarm. Don't set yourself up for failure, set the alarm for a time where you get at least 6 hours of sleep and you know you can get up. Your body will normally wake you up when it's time to get up, if its 15 minutes before the alarm, don't say "*I still have 15 minutes of sleep*," just get up. We go through waves of sleep, from light sleep, to deep sleep, to REM, alternating back and forth throughout the night. I recommend an UP band by Jawbone or a Fitbit. They have a gentle vibrating alarm that wakes you up during your light sleep stage. Have you ever gotten a full night sleep but still felt groggy? We all have, and it's not that you overslept, it's simply because we woke up during an REM cycle or deep state of sleep. When you wake up on your own, 15 minutes before that alarm goes off, it is because you were in a light state, its perfect, just get up. If you hit the snooze you will fall back asleep, and if you are in a state of deep sleep when that alarm goes off again, you will feel tired and groggy all day. Honor that first commitment, practice the small discipline, No Snooze.

Make Your Bed

If you make your bed every morning you will have accomplished your second small discipline or task of the day. It will give you a small sense of pride and give you that lift you need to start your day. It can help propel you forward in knocking out another task, and then another, and another. By days' end that one task will have turned into many tasks and your day will be filled with accomplishment. It will also reinforce that even the little things in life matter, if you can't do the simple little tasks right than how will you do the big things. Worst case scenario, even if you don't get anything else done for the day, you come home and are reminded that you paid attention to detail, you did accomplish something, you did practice self-discipline, and it will provide you the satisfaction you need right before you go to bed.

I AM

I AM… a man of faith

I AM… a man of character

I AM… an avid learner

I AM... a master of influence.

I was once asked a simple question, it was what seemed an easy question, but it ended up being a profound life changer for me. The question was... Who are you? I was asked to answer in the I AM format.

I am Alex Alfaro... *"no you're not, that's just your name."*

I am the owner of SCL Group... *"That's your occupation, not who you are."*

I am a man... *"that's your gender not who you are."*

It was very difficult at first, especially when someone is standing in front of you waiting for an answer, watching your tone, and watching your body language to see if you believe what you are saying. Eventually I ended up with my top 4 which I stated above. It can be who you are, or who you want to become. I recommend you find at least 4 and repeat them daily. Stand in front of the mirror and speak them in the morning, repeat them a few times throughout the day, and right before you go to bed. This simple daily discipline will help program your subconscious with positive affirmations and help you maintain PMA. You need to know who you are and who you want to become before you can ever get there.

Meditation

I have learned and regularly practice a technique called Transcendental Meditation or TM. It is taught one on one, and the simple technique is effortless and easy. You practice 2 times a day for 20 minutes and the technique is easy to learn and easy to master. You get results instantly after your first mediation. If you want more information and want to learn the technique you can go to www.TM.org there are centers located all over the world. Meditation relaxes and recharges the mind and body, it creates a brighter and a more positive state of mind. Personally, it gives me energy, vitality, and a sense of clarity. There are hundreds of published research studies that have found that TM is highly effective on stress and anxiety, brain function, and cardiovascular health. Since I have started meditating my caffeine intake has drastically been reduced to almost zero. I now drink coffee for the flavor and for the positive emotion I get from its aroma. With energy and vitality, it's almost impossible to not feel great and maintain a positive mental attitude. People like Jerry Seinfeld, Ellen DeGeneres, Russel Simons, Jay Z, Tom Brady, Steven Spielberg and many more athletes, actors and producers swear by it. These are all high achievers, performing at the highest levels in their field, so when I listen for wisdom, I always make sure it's from a respected source. It was at the very least worth a try for me, and this simple and effortless daily discipline has paid dividends in my life.

WED (Water, Exercise, Diet)

I use the acronym WED and on Wednesday I am reminded to evaluate my water, exercise and diet for the week. It is very difficult to maintain a positive mental attitude when you're constantly sick, out of shape and overweight and without energy and vitality. I have been into health and fitness since I was 21 years old. I have tried many different workout plans and studied and practiced many diets and cleanses. What I have found is that simple is better. It is not difficult to start living a healthy lifestyle and get into shape. All it takes is another few simple small disciplines performed consistently. Whenever I am asked about diets or exercise I always start with water, then get into exercise, and finish with a healthy diet. I recommend 32oz of water for every 50lbs of body weight. Yes, it sounds like a ton of water but remember, that's the goal. You don't have to start there; your small daily discipline should simply be 32oz per day and you can gradually increase from there. Water flushes out the toxins from your system and balances out the acidity in the body. The more alkaline the body is, the more efficient and effective your immune system, digestive system, and metabolism will work. If you get your digestive system and metabolism functioning at peak you will begin to feel better, think better, sleep better and lose weight. All this without changing your exercise or what you eat.

Once you have developed the discipline of drinking water then you can shift the focus to exercise. Make sure you get at least 10,000 steps in per day. It's not that difficult to do, just choose that parking space further away instead of circling around for the closest one, walk to the local store instead of driving, or simply jump on that treadmill that's been collecting dust in the garage. This daily discipline is simple and effective. If you have already developed the habit of drinking water, then you have noticed those extra steps to your daily routine, simply by having to go to the restroom ever 20 minutes.

Finally, we can look at a healthy diet. Once we have spent the time establishing these first two daily disciplines water and exercise (steps), and these disciplines have become habits, we can then shift are full attention to what we eat. You will have already noticed that because of the water consciousness, you have chosen water instead of soft drinks, or other sugary drinks during your meals. You have noticed that your portions are smaller because the water keeps your stomach feeling full. You have already established a healthier diet without changing what you eat. Our choices are limited when it comes to healthy foods available at restaurants and our local fast food place. You should simply focus on making sure you get the nutrients you need daily, I like to focus on the greens. I use a product called PH Miracle Super Greens that I add to my first 2- 32oz bottles of water for the day. I learned about this product on the Living Health Audiobook by Tony Robbins, and it can be found at www.pmhlife.com. It helps you get the greens and nutrients you need daily. Please note that I do not get paid for any of these recommendations for products, these are just products that I use after years of trial and error of many similar items. When it comes to a healthy diet, make the daily discipline is easy, simply make sure you at least have one healthy and nutritious meal per day. I recommend it to be your breakfast, a healthy green juice flooded with vitamins and minerals in the morning is ideal. Your body has been fasting overnight and working its way back to optimal peak performance, the first meal, or the break of the fast, should be fuel to energize and revitalize. A green juice consisting of Parsley, Spinach, Kale, Celery, Cucumber, Lemon and Apple is perfect.

Read Books & Listen to Audios

One of my most important daily disciplines for a positive mental attitude and how I started my journey to reading daily and listening to audios happened a few years after the worst turmoil of my life. I picked up the book "*Think and Grow Rich*" by Napoleon Hill for the second time in my life in 2012, 4 years after I had suffered through the housing meltdown. I lost multiple properties in 2008 and by the end of 2009 I had run through all my savings. Not only that, but amid trying to save it all, I made the biggest mistake of accumulating a ton of debt. I went from living in a 2500sqft home to living in a 150sqft bedroom at my brother in laws 900sqft home. My life became the mundane, I was driving 45 minutes each way to a job, and living paycheck to paycheck, making just enough to survive. I continued to default on my debt and wasn't even close to living the lifestyle I had become so accustomed to. My mindset was negative, I felt it had it all been a fluke, and in my head, I would never amount to anything. My confidence was at an all-time low. It all turned around the day I noticed the book "*Think and Grow Rich*" sitting in one of the boxes. I picked it up and started spending my free time reading instead of watching television or playing video games. I turned my 45-minute drive of misery to an institution of higher education. I felt an immediate shift in mindset and my world and reality began to change once again. The daily discipline is one simple page a day. If you read one page of a positive and inspirational book each day, you will develop a growth mindset. One page of reading and you are already better then you where the day before. That one page will become one chapter, and that one chapter can become a book a month. In a year's time, you will have read more books than the

If You Change Your Thinking You Change Your Reality

average American, who doesn't even pick up another book after high school or college. If you are not a reader, keep it simple at first, pick up a book with a daily devotional that gives you a page to read for each day of the year. My favorite is the Daily Stoic by Ryan Holiday or Napoleon Hill's Daily Inspiration for all Seasons. It will hold you accountable to your daily reading. Use your free time to listen to audios. Don't waste any time... don't waste your drive to work, don't waste your time waiting in lines or waiting for meals, play an audiobook, even in the background while working, let your subconscious go to work.

A growth mindset has worked for me, and it will always be about daily growth. You are either growing or dying, it's your choice. No Snooze, Make Your Bed, I AM, Meditation, WED (Water, Exercise, Diet), Read Books and Listen to Audios. These are 6 of my personal daily disciplines in which I practice without fail every single day. They are simple, easy, and effective. They drastically shifted my mindset and altered the course of my life, and I am sure they can impact yours. You get what you think about most...so why not think about, and focus on all the positives of the world. To successfully play this game of life one must have full control of one's mind. If you can imagine only good, you will bring into your life every righteous desire of your heart, - Health, Wealth, Love, Friendships, Perfect Self Expression and the Highest Ideals. Think about and admire the beauty of nature and its laws, the good in all the people you meet, and the best qualities in your friends and family.

> *"Keep thy heart (or imagination) with all diligence, for out of it are the issues of life."*
>
> — Proverbs 4:23

This means that what you imagine, sooner or later you externalize in your life. Your mindset is the key to your happiness, when I learned this my world drastically changed yet everything in it remained the same.

BIO | Alex Alfaro

Alex Alfaro is the CEO and Founder of SCL Group, a Supply Chain and Logistics Consulting Firm. He is the managing partner of StuDoc, a student loan consolidation call center focused on consolidating loans into government programs and helping people eliminate student loan debt.

He is a personal fitness trainer through the National Academy of Sports Medicine, Certified Instructor for the Napoleon Hill Foundation, and Master Practitioner of NLP-Neuro Linguistic Programming.

Throughout his study in the of Napoleon Hill's Success Philosophy he was able to turn adversity and failure into success and both his companies, SCL Group and StuDoc are now multimillion dollar revenue firms.

Inspired by Napoleon Hill's *"Think and Grow Rich"* and the 17 Laws of Success he formed SMA a non-profit organization. Stoic Mastermind Alliance focuses on PMA (Positive Mental

Attitude), teaches the 17 Laws of Success, NLP-Neuro Linguistic Programming as taught by the founder Richard Bandler, and Stoicism an ancient Stoic Philosophy that pursues self-mastery, perseverance and contains some of the greatest wisdom in the history of the world.

CHAPTER 11

Your Success Puzzle

By: Gary Burleson

Going to Jail

While completing my certification process as an instructor of the Napoleon Hill Science of Success, I have been teaching the Keys to Success in the Morgan County State Prison in Wartburg, Tennessee, in association with The FOCUS Prison Ministry and The Napoleon Hill Foundation. I have taught the class for three years for a total of five times. It has been very rewarding to me, and, also to the men who have gone through the class. This is totally a volunteer venture with no financial compensation.

At first it seemed awkward to be talking to men who may be imprisoned for another five to ten years or more about their Definite Major Purpose in life, taking possession of their minds, living the rewards of a life set on a course and purpose, overcoming the odds of failure and defeat, and learning, growing, and experiencing the life of a person in charge and successful. All these guys want when they are released is to be reunited with their families, find a job, and survive without resorting to crime again.

I had a gentleman come up to me after he completed the course to say how, at first, he was despondent and depressed about his life and future; but when he read the chapter on positive mental attitude his outlook on life changed. Wayne Dyer says, *"When you begin to look at things differently, then the things you look at begin to change.*" This is what happened. He began to associate with other people in the class who had similar feelings of hope and desire for a better future. He replaced the negative self-defeating thoughts with positive affirming thoughts. Now he has the keys to unlock the doors of opportunity, hope, and a bright future.

One day, as I stood in the middle of this 54 man class, (they were seated in a horseshoe shape and I would walk in the middle of it) talking to them face to face, an idea came to me. These were minimum security risk men, and I never felt threatened or fearful. Most of them were very friendly and truly grateful that I came to teach them and were very receptive to the information. On this one occasion, an inspired thought came to me as I was talking. An image of a puzzle and the puzzle box. The words just came out of my mouth, "*Life is like a puzzle, you may have all the pieces, but if you don't have a clear picture of what is on the cover of the puzzle box, it will be very difficult, if not impossible, to put the puzzle together.*" I went on to explain how important it is to have a vision for their lives, an explicitly clear image of the life they want. The clearer the image the easier it will be to assemble or manifest. Think about it, when you're putting a puzzle together how often do you look at the picture on the box cover, just about every piece, right? Well, this is how we build a life. We may have the knowledge, i.e., the pieces of the puzzle, but unless we have a clear vision, i.e., an image to work with, we will spend time futilely. At this point is when most people surrender to despair and the negative messages associated with that mindset - like I can't do this, it's too hard, I'm not smart enough, it's too expensive, I'll never be able to do this, and on-and-on the negative self-talk goes.

Immediately I was astonished at my words and later wrote them down, thinking, this could be a good way to market my services. I created my business with the same name Your Success Puzzle Solved.

The "I Am Factor"

Another topic I talk about is *"The I Am Factortm"*. It's basically an exercise the men do. On a sheet of paper, they write on every line the words *"I am."* Then after those two words something positive about themselves, like I am a good father, or I am a hard worker, or I am an honest person. You get the point. Sometimes they find it hard to think of anything positive about themselves, so I give them ideas, and then it's like *"Oh, yeah."* I explain that *whatever follows these two words (I am) will determine the rest of their lives.* The thoughts you think and how you feel about yourself will be evident in the results you are getting. If you are thinking *"I could never do that"* or *"What will people think of me?"* you are stifling your growth as a creative being, and you are limiting your God given talents and abilities that will move you forward in life. That person is living in the negative flow of the river of life as Napoleon describes it. That person has not taken possession of his mind and is living out the penalties of not doing so. I'll talk about that more later. So, they had better get a positive image of themselves and live up to it.

Many of us have poor self-esteem and poor self-images. So many of us, even those of us who seemingly have productive and happy lives free of jail and confinement, think negatively of ourselves and allow negative messages to loop over and over in our heads like *"I'm not worthy of the good that might happen,"* and we discount our value, our talents and our abilities. Most of these guys in jail do have really damaged egos and self-esteem. They have been told all their lives what a failure they are, what a disappointment they are, how stupid they are, that they'll never amount to anything except being a criminal. These are the messages they've heard over and over, and they believe and live them out. But, during the course of these negative onslaughts to their precious hearts that God gave them at birth, which have been hurt repeatedly, they have had no other recourse than to protect their hearts by covering them over and over with bandages like an onion covers its core so their precious hearts are protected. Now it has been covered and concealed and unfortunately lost and forgotten. The heart loses its feelings and becomes numb to any further belittlements, insults, and criticisms. They no longer feel except to hate, fight, and hurt others. These are the negative motives and feelings that bring on negative results. They must learn how to replace those negative thoughts and feelings with positive ones. They must get a positive image of themselves.

Your most valuable possession

I have a glass diamond; it's four inches in diameter in a clear acrylic case. It's fascinating and amazing to look at this beautiful stone and wish upon it. I hold it up and tell them that "*this diamond is the most rare and valuable gemstone in the world.*" It is just like your hearts, it is valuable, precious and rare, unique, a one of a kind. It is in the case for all to see, and then I say words like what they've heard all their lives, "*you're worthless,*" and I throw some dirt in the case, and I'll repeat these negative messages until the gem is covered and can no longer be seen. It is concealed and no longer available to admire. This is what we do to our hearts over time in order to protect them, and now they are soiled, dirty, unclean and must be unearthed. I tell them that it's time to go treasure hunting. That they must discover again how precious, unique, rare, talented and gifted they are. They have to discover their true selves, as they were meant to be. They must become acquainted with their "*other selves*". All the layers of protection must be peeled away, and we have to give our hearts to God who created them and ask Him to restore them and transform them into the once original pure form they were when we were born. I believe this is where we need to be if we are to find a true and lasting peace, love for ourselves, and live a life of abundance and success. A pure heart is as integral a piece of the success puzzle as all the others. Also, loving and taking care of one's self both mentally and physically. We have to stop hating ourselves and self-sabotaging because of our "*sins.*"

    All of these positive messages are hopefully getting through and making an impression on their minds, hearts, and souls.

Positive messages and autosuggestions are what we need to replace the negative messages that so naturally come to us. We must deliberately inject the positives into our subconscious minds.

What is PMA?

Getting back to positive mental attitude; we all know what positive means. It's the opposite of negative, and we all know what negative is. I've given plenty of examples of negative thus far. But what is mental attitude? We have to break it down into its two components - mental and attitude.

Mental is mind, and what is mind? I'll give you a hint, it's not the grey matter in your head. We all naturally think of that, but our brain is no more a part of mind than our fingers or toes.

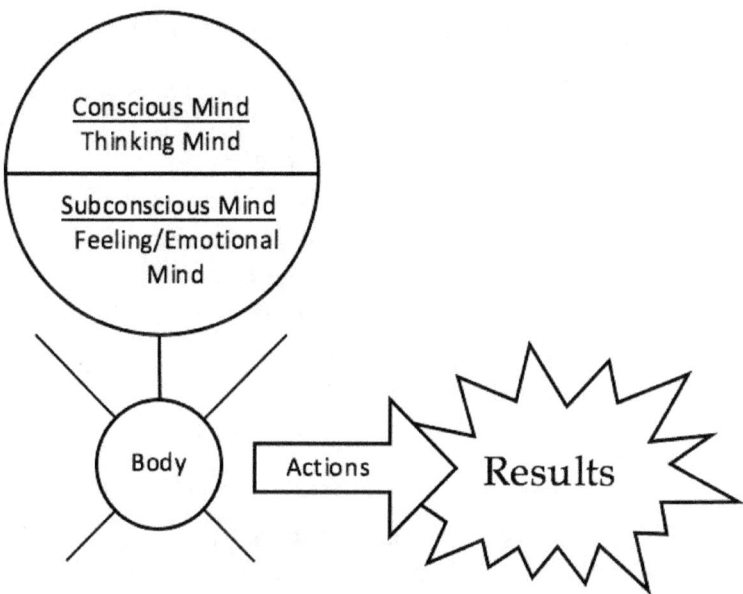

Let me give you example. Since we think in images it would be easier to describe using an illustration. Our mind is made up of our conscious mind or the thinking mind. It is also consists of our subconscious mind or our feeling/emotional mind. Our thoughts and our feelings move our bodies, which is also a part of mind. We move and act as we've been conditioned from birth and manifest results. We show our attitude whether positive or negative based on the results we manifest.

And what is attitude? Attitude is a combination of your thoughts, feelings, and actions. It's easy to see someone's attitude and the nature of their mind by their actions and the manifested results. <u>Our minds and attitudes are one</u>. It would behoove one to have a positive mental attitude if one wants to see positive results. So we have to change or transform our minds from the old paradigms (ways of doing things/ thinking) to new positive, affirming, faith-based paradigms rather than fear-based paradigms. Every time you catch yourself thinking negatively, say to yourself, "*NO!*" I will not believe that thought, I choose to believe "*I can!,*" "*I will,*" because I AM……. And what follows that determines how you will live the rest of your life, hence, The I Am Factotum.

Napoleon Hill says in *Think and Grow Rich* in the chapter on the subconscious mind that,

> *"The negatives automatically inject themselves into the thought impulses, which ensures their passage into the subconscious mind. The positives must be injected, through the principle of autosuggestion into the thought impulses which an individual wishes to pass on to his or her subconscious mind."*

The same goes for our thoughts. We become what we think about. Napoleon Hill says that our thoughts are the only things we have complete and absolute control over. He says in the epilogue of *Think and Grow Rich*, "We have absolute control over but one thing, and that is our thoughts. This is the most significant and inspiring of all known facts! It reflects the divine nature of humanity. This divine prerogative is the sole means by which you may control your own destiny. If you fail to control your own mind, you may be sure you will control nothing else." And also *"Mind control is a result of self-discipline and habit. You either control your mind or it controls you."* Then he states, *"The most practical of all methods for controlling the mind is the habit of keeping it busy with a definite purpose backed by a definite plan."*

      No one else can control our thoughts, our feelings, or our actions unless we allow it. This is easier said than done, because from birth, our teachers, parents, society, media, etc., have influenced our thoughts and our feelings for right and wrong, for truth and injustice. We learned with our five senses: what we see, hear, smell, taste or touch, and our paradigms were set. But we have intellectual faculties, and we must begin to exercise these for our advantage, these being perception, intuition, will, imagination, reason and memory. Because of the constraints of the length of this chapter, I will have to leave the explanations of these faculties to a rather brief explanation. Perception is how we view our world around us, and how we perceive ourselves; Intuition is our ability to discern circumstances as either beneficial or not; our Will is the ability to focus or refocus from all the distractions; Imagination is our ability to create, or solve. The ability to Reason deductively and inductively is a gift only humans enjoy, and our Memory, we remember everything, we may not remember what we had for breakfast or someone's name we just heard, but we remember all sense impressions made on our minds both positive and negative over the years. We must begin to use theses faculties to analyze our thoughts and our feelings as to their validity and whether they are moving us in a positive direction to a positive end or a negative direction to a negative end.

The Rewards

So, here are the rewards of taking possession of our minds; a success consciousness, sound health, both mental and physical, financial independence, a labor of love with which to express yourself, peace of mind, applied faith which makes fear impossible, enduring friendships, longevity, a well-balanced life, immunity from self-limitation, and the wisdom to understand yourself and others. Have you taken possession of your mind or are you living out the penalties? Here are the penalties of not taking possession of your mind; poverty and misery your entire life, mental and physical ailments, self-limitations which trap you in mediocrity, fear and all of its destructive consequences, hatred of the means by which you support yourself, many enemies and few friends, every brand of worry known to humanity, being a victim of every negative influence you encounter, subjection to the will of others, and a wasted life which does nothing to better the human condition. You may also know someone who is living out the penalties, many of us do. The men I teach in class are perfect examples of those who haven't taken possession of their minds, or think accurately for themselves, which is another piece of the success puzzle - accurate thinking. Our thoughts must not only be positive, but they must also be accurately based on facts and truth, not hearsay or opinions, or superstition.

Possessing and owning our thoughts is hard work and a constant battle at first. Over time, though, this habit of thinking becomes much easier, and keeping our minds in a positive attitude and rejecting negative thoughts and influences becomes second nature. It's something like working out. You have muscles, which become atrophied when not used or exercised. Our mental muscles, so to speak, need exercise also to become strengthened. Once they reach a certain level, it's all about maintaining. Personal development is exercise. Reading is personal development and how we grow, learn and change. It must be a lifelong habit or we will become atrophic. But it's how we enjoy the rewards of taking possession of our minds.

So, what's your motivation? Napoleon Hill lists ten primary motives all of us have that influence our behavior. These are: the desire for material gain, the desire for self-expression and recognition, the desire for freedom of body and mind, the emotion of love, the emotion of fear, the emotion of sex or passion, the desire for life after death, the emotion of hate, the emotion of revenge, and the desire for self-preservation. Most of these, or a combination, affect all of us to one degree or another, and they are connected to our definite purpose in life. Another major piece of the success puzzle is your definite major purpose in life.

Myself, like many of us, drifted into my career. One thing led to another and I did what needed doing to earn income. My father was a homebuilder, so this gave me the opportunity to work on construction sites. Because of a lack of guidance, I learned the home building trade by default. It wasn't what I really wanted to do, but it was what I learned. After obtaining a general contractor's license, and building houses for four years, I found it extremely stressful and I hated it. It was a result of not taking possession of my mind. I was miserable. Then I got into the custom closet trade. One day I was walking away from a job thinking, *"I've earned money with a hammer and a nail for the last 30 years. I don't want to do this for the next 30. I want to earn my income with a microphone and an ink pen."* So, I decided then and there to start over and remake myself. Over the next ten years, I worked my job while learning to become a certified Life Success Consultant and a certified instructor by the Napoleon Hill Foundation. I also became a member of Toastmasters, an International Public Speaking and Leadership organization. Having invested countless hours and much money in seminars, workshops, books, and courses to become my *"other self."* There was a very strong desire to become this.

I love helping people to believe and be aware that their dreams are also attainable and achievable, for "whatever the mind can conceive and believe it can achieve." I had to maintain a positive mental attitude for a long time - to believe and apply my faith, my money, and my energy - sacrificing at many levels and persevering one day at a time for years. It wasn't easy. It was very difficult and trying, but I *"arrived."*

My two most favorite paragraphs in *Think and Grow Rich* are these: "*You may have been disappointed, you may have suffered setbacks and defeat during hard economic times, you may have felt the great heart within you crushed until it bled. Take courage, for these experiences have tempered the spiritual metal of which you are made - they are assets of incomparable value".*

Remember, too, that all who succeed in life get off to a bad start and pass through many heartbreaking struggles before they "*arrive.*" The turning point in the lives of those who succeed usually comes at the moment of some crisis, through which they are introduced to their "*other selves.*" The reason many people fail is mainly because they give up before they "*arrive.*" They begin to focus on the negative images and messages in their minds they have heard all their lives rather than replacing them with positive affirming messages and a clear image of their success puzzle. Therefore it is so important to have in writing your definite major purpose, and to read it out loud twice daily with as much emotion and belief as you can, visualizing, owning and possessing in your mind the desired end result.

If that desire isn't a white-hot fire it will not endure the failures and defeats, the criticisms, and doubts, the sidetracks and roadblocks of all kinds. The focusing and refocusing over and over again endlessly in pursuit of that destination will make it a journey seemingly too far or difficult to complete. It will seem too complicated, and require too much energy, just like an ordinary puzzle. Success takes the kind of commitment that many aren't willing to endure. It takes discipline and persistence in going the extra mile, it requires teamwork, and a mastermind alliance, enthusiasm and controlled attention. It takes creative vision and a pleasing personality in addition to a positive mental attitude. Everyone must learn from their failures and defeats, by finding the equal and opposite value and lesson in them, and never, never, never, never quit.

Believe me when I say, it's worth it, and if I can do it, there's no excuse that you can't achieve your dreams and goals as well.

Believe.

BIO | Gary Burleson

Gary Burleson is certified by The Napoleon Hill Foundation to teach the *PMA: Science of Success* course, and is certified by Bob Proctor as a Life Success Consultant. Gary has also been a Toastmaster for the last 15 years. Gary has published a workbook, the first in a series, entitled

A Philosophy for Personal Achievement: Principle #8 Persistence based on Napoleon Hill's book *Think and Grow Rich*, which he uses in the workshops he conducts for companies and in coaching for individuals.

Gary is a dynamic speaker and teacher of the Napoleon Hill Philosophy of Personal Achievement and Science of Success. Gary has been teaching these principles in classes as a volunteer with The FOCUS Prison Ministry in the Morgan County State Prison and The Knox County Detention Facility for the last six years on Tuesdays. Gary jokingly says Tuesday is his day to "go to jail".

As a Life Success Consultant Gary understands The Mind and the paradigms that control our very lives and the RESULTS we get because of them, and that true transformation begins in our mind and our heart.

The day Gary took possession of his mind he decided that he would remake himself, that he would become an author, a speaker and a coach. Today Gary is helping young adults, and inmates, starting out in life, start out with a solid foundation of knowledge and resources that they didn't learn about in public schools or in their homes, namely the Napoleon Hill Success Principles. Likewise, with older men and women, who also like Gary, need or want to remake themselves and follow their passions. Gary has learned from his experiences, the ins- and- outs, the pros and cons, the roadblocks to avoid and the "secrets" to achieving ones Definite Major Purpose in life, and is in a unique position to help those who believe, that their dreams are also attainable and achievable. Gary truly believes that *"Whatever the mind can conceive and believe it can achieve"*, and Gary truly believes he can help you achieve your dreams and goals.

Gary can be reached through his website http://yoursuccesspuzzle.com or by email at gary.burleson@yoursuccesspuzzle.com

CHAPTER 12

Positive Mental Attitude

By: Ann McNeill

There is power in positive thinking, but there is also power in negative thinking. Thinking negatively has more detrimental effects than you know. What we think is actually reflected in our facial expressions and reflects in our attitudes. Attitude is inward thinking expressed by outward behavior. You cannot think negative thoughts and have a beautiful smile on your face. You cannot be thinking beautiful thoughts and have a frown on your face. Your mind is like a computer - junk in, junk out. Your thoughts, emotions, and facial expressions go hand-in-hand; but more important than that is the fact that when you entertain negative, disappointing, or evil thoughts, your body begins to weaken. It sinks into a position that causes sickness and disease. To renew your body, you must beautify your mind with positive thinking. Negative thoughts of unforgiveness, hatred, guilt, shame, and bitterness rob the body of its vitality and health. You must monitor your thinking in order to be truly successful. Your attitude will also affect your courage to pursue a worthy goal. If you are doubtful or fearful, you will not even try to go after something you inwardly desire. King David was a perfect example of how a fearless attitude can bring forth courage. Courage is required for a positive mental attitude. When it came to killing a Philistine giant who was constantly mocking, intimidating, and embarrassing the Israelites, forty-thousand Israelite soldiers all thought, *"Goliath is so big that we can never kill him"* But David looked at the same giant and thought, "*Goliath is so big that there is no way I can miss him.*" His attitude bred his courage! You can not miss a target or a goal you set, once you understand how to turn your defeat and fear into desires for something better, using your positive mental attitude.

The Day My Mind Became Elevated

We all are where we are because of where our thoughts have brought us, and we will be in the future where our thoughts take us. Sometimes it takes the right motivation to elevate your thoughts into a realm where you will be determined to enhance your life through positive thinking supplemented by positive action. For me, that motivation came on December 31, 1979 when my dream began to unfold. I was 25 years old, married, and had one child. It was New Year's Eve, and my husband and friends had gone out to bring in the New Year. I had decided to stay home to begin reading my new book *Think and Grow Rich* by Napoleon Hill. As I began to read the book, the book began to read me! That book changed my life and started me on a journey towards pursuing higher goals and deeper aspirations. When I reached page 36, there were four questions requiring me, the reader to answer. I took my pen and pad and eagerly attempted to answer each question. These questions started me on a new journey towards mind renewal and mental elevation. The questions read as follows:

Six ways to turn Desires into Gold:

The method by which desire for riches can be transmuted into its financial equivalent, consists of six definite, practical steps:

First: Fix in your mind the exact amount of money you desire. It is not sufficient nearly to say, "*I want plenty of money*". Be definite as to the amount (there is a psychological reason for definiteness, which will be described in a subsequent chapter).

Second: Determine exactly what you intend to give in return for the money (there is no such reality as, *"something for nothing."*)

Third: Establish a definite date when you intend to posses the money you desire.

Fourth: Create a definite plan for carrying out your desire, and begin at once, whether you are ready or not to put this plan into action.

Fifth: Write out a clear, concise statement of the amount of money you intend to acquire. Name the time limit for its acquisition. State what you intend to give in return for the money and describe clearly the plan through which you intent to accumulate it.

Six: Read your written statement aloud, twice daily, once just before retiring at night, and once after arising in the morning. As you read, see and feel and believe yourself already in possession of the money.

After reading *Think and Grow Rich* in 1979, I identified $1,000, as the amount of money I had identified in step one. To date, everything I endeavored from a business standpoint was predicated on employing the six steps to turn desires into riches. Reading *'Think & Grow Rich'* helped me to realize that in this life, we must *"give"* in order to *"get"*. My mindset embraced the principles of identifying what is desired, identifying what will be given in exchange for my desire, identifying a definite date for the acquisition of my desire, creating a definite plan for my desire, identifying the timeline and repeating the affirmation about this desire daily in order to train my subconsciousness into being ready to receive it, with a positive mental attitude. Since December 31, 1979, I am still using the principles because they have proven to work. I share the principles with all who will listen and I continuously cultivate positive thinking, which is a necessity for bringing your vision out of the mental realm into the natural realm.

Thoughts are Things

Everything you are, everything you do, everywhere you go, the decisions you make, the job that you have, and even the clothes that you wear first originated in your mind. What you see in the material form had two births. First, there was the mental birth where the thought was conceived. Then, there was the physical birth when the thoughts materialized. For example, if your mind tells you that you are hungry and are craving pizza that is the first birth. You then begin to desire pizza so much that you can taste it. After the pizza is delivered or after you go and pick it up, your thought has then become the thing. Thoughts are things. The thought was pulled out of the mental realm and brought into the natural realm. The book that you are reading right now was first a thought. Everything has two births.

If we know that thoughts are things, then why should we not begin to strategically conceive thoughts and purposefully allow them to become things? Recognize the thoughts that are worthy of attention because some are not worth entertaining and must be dismissed. Some thoughts that come to us are fruitless and foolish. I still get outlandish and foolish thoughts that come to me and when I recognize them, I say to myself, *"Where in the world did that come from?"* Then, I simply release it. Other thoughts can be negative and destructive. They too must be dismissed. Just because you receive such thoughts does not mean that you are a bad person. Everyone receives negative thoughts - everyone! …but it is the wise person who recognizes the bad thoughts and eradicates them. We constantly pick up the thoughts of others from their vibrations. Sometimes thoughts come to our minds and we think they belong to us when they really have come from others. These thoughts linger in the invisible realm looking for an outlet of expression. When you release them from your mind, they continue to linger until another mind picks them up and acts on them.

The key is to recognize those that will bear no positive fruit and evict them immediately! When negative, dishonest, sinister thoughts enter your mind and you entertain them, they feel comfortable returning, so they do. As you continue to entertain them a second and a third time, they begin seeking an outlet of expression through you. Thoughts are things, so as soon as an opportunity to materialize appears, the negative thought becomes a thing. Those negative, deceitful, sinister thoughts manifest and become a cause. After you have initiated the cause, you must be prepared for the effect that will result. Thoughts are seeds, and when planted in the mind, then cultivated and watered, will bring forth a harvest. The harvest will either be good or bad. It is up to you and is based upon the nature of the seed sown. Other thoughts are of a positive nature, such as when it hits you to do something nice for someone for no particular reason. Sometimes your mind tells you to call a certain person just to see how they are doing. Those thoughts are good seeds and will return a good harvest. Where there is a cause, there will also be an effect. Other thoughts are actual ideas that come out of the mind of the Creator and are then released into the earth realm to human minds. The mind that picks up the idea should not entertain it momentarily then forget about it, but that mind must cultivate and nurture the idea until it materializes. When steps are taken for the manifestation of the idea to occur, that person will get the reward.

How Desires Become Reality

Idealization, Visualization, and Manifestation. This is the order in which your desires become a reality. Whether you realize it or not, your life is shaped by the images you have seen and entertained in your mind over the years. You may have consciously entertained these images through mental exercises such as meditation, or unconsciously entertained the images through daydreaming; but you are the one who brought them out of the invisible (your mind) into the visible (your environment) and you are the one who are now dealing with the existence of these thoughts in your life whether they are good or bad. Therefore, it is imperative that you become consciously aware of the thoughts, imaginations and visions that you entertain on a day to day basis because what you think about today shall become the reality that you will experience tomorrow, just as what you are experiencing today, is the reality of what you thought about in the past. What came to you in the physical world is what already existed in your inner world. When you consistently envision yourself as having self-actualized, meaning you have achieved your highest dreams and are living the life you always desired while possessing peace, harmony, abundance, and an even flow of love going out and coming in, then you are bringing your highest ideal to you. If you are not yet living your highest ideal, but you can "see" yourself as living this ideal through strategic visualization, then you are on the road to manifestation and will soon kiss the lips of your desires. When you visualize your ideal on a consistent basis through meditation, you are actually using the law of cause and effect.

Thinking and Acting

Like King David, since 1979 I have found a way to use my positive mental attitude to deal with many giants in my life and in my businesses. These experiences are teaching me the differences between thinking and acting on my thoughts. I am blessed and grateful to have learned such lessons early in life. Everyone everywhere thinks and acts every day. If you are not thinking and acting; then you are not living. You are only existing. Even if you are ignorant of this fact, you are still changing for better or worse. We can become masters of ourselves because we have the power to control our thoughts. We must get ourselves right by monitoring our way of thinking. Weak are they who allow their thoughts to control their actions; strong are they who force their actions to control their thoughts.

    I opened this chapter discussing the challenges of where my negative thinking had brought me prior to reading '*Think & Grow Rich*'. I want to end this chapter by sharing the impact and results of employing the habit of a positive mental attitude in all situations. My initial goal, after reading '*Think & Grow Rich*' was to save $1,000 a year. That was back in 1979. That goal was achieved. After creating many for-profit and not for-profit businesses, my goal now is to save $1,000 passive income per week, and teaching others how to live a better quality of life while maximizing their gifts. Take charge of your thoughts. Let your mind feast upon the things that will bring you peace, joy, happiness, love, prosperity, success and abundance. You have the power to master your mind. Now take control. Everything is in your hands. Just like King David, you can hit the target with a positive mental attitude.

BIO | Ann McNeill

Ann McNeill is President/CEO of one of South Florida's few African American-female owned construction companies. McNeill Construction (MCO) was founded 40 years ago and is still one of the leading minority firms in South Florida in the area of construction management and project controls. MCO construction has worked on the majority of the flagship projects in South Florida, such as The Miami Airlines Arena, The Marlins Ballpark, The Miami International Airport, The Miami Science Museum, The Miami Children's Courthouse and many more.

Demonstrative of being a female licensed general contractor, Ann discovered that women in the construction business were far and few between. She strongly believed that a network of women in construction needed to be created. As a result, Ann started The National Association of Black Women in Construction (NABWIC). The association was created to help build a pipeline for black women in the public sector, black women in the private sector, black women entrepreneurs and young ladies in school. The objective of the school component is for Black girls to study STEM (Science, Technology, Engineering and Mathematics) in middle school, high school and college who may have a desire to enter the construction industry at all levels - from the trades to management and ownership. The main purpose of NABWIC is to create a network of professional women in the construction industry who teach each other how to turn contacts into contracts. This is done through a *"Billion Dollar Luncheon"*, which is held each month. As a result of her track record of accomplishments, Ann has been featured in Black Enterprise Magazine, USA Today and ABC's World News.

She is also President of MCO Consulting, Inc., a consulting company that provides outreach, monitoring and compliance for private sector firms that work on public sector land. She has received numerous awards and recognitions for her work in her industry and also in the community. She received her Bachelor's Degree in accounting from Florida Memorial College (University) and her Master's Degree in finance from Barry University. She is married to Daniel McNeill and has two daughters, Danelle and Ionnie. She also has one grandson, Malachi and a granddaughter, Rajahnia.

CHAPTER 13

To Whom Much is Given Much Is Required

By: Linda (Nefertiti) Patton

For most of my life, the scripture Luke 12:48 *ONLY* meant, if you were rich or successful or had a lot of stuff, *MUCH* was required of you. Today it takes on a whole new meaning. I've had a lot of *STUFF* in my life and I realize that much IS required of me! The requirement is for me to share the events of my life and show how a **Positive Mental Attitude** and **Applied Faith** has made it possible for me to keep going, even when I wanted to give up! I am no longer a victim I am an *OVERCOMER*!

I grew up in Detroit, Michigan at a very precarious time for people of color. Consequently, my childhood was full of adversity that forced me to grow up quickly.

I survived being molested by one of my teachers in elementary school at a time in my life where my biggest concern should have been recess! My teacher was Caucasian and warned me no one would believe that he would touch a *N-word girl*. Sadly, even though my mother went to school with the intention of setting them straight for violating one of her children, I was labeled as a troublemaker and that was only the beginning! My mother walked out of the school *beaten down* and called me a troublemaker as well. My teacher mysteriously ended up going to work at another school after my mother reported the incident. Today I understand the dynamics of what happened. I didn't understand as a child, but I appreciate what my mother had to go through on my behalf.

My father was my first **Mentor**; he was self-employed. I never saw him work for another man! My first goal in life was to work for myself. My mother was a stay at home mom, and with a large family. It was rough making ends meet. Although my father worked most of the time he made sure he spent as much quality time with his children as he could. My mother did not drive so my father took us everywhere we went. He would take us to Belle Isle, a popular park in Detroit. On occasion he would take us *out of the country to Canada.* We would either travel over the Ambassador Bridge or through the tunnel. We would go to Rondeau Bay, Ontario with its white sand beaches or Horseback riding in Canada. Daddy would take us to a popular restaurant in Detroit called Dot and Etta's Shrimp (*I still love Shrimp*)! For special occasions he would bring home a Caramel Cake (*one of my favorites*)! He would drive us to Arkansas to visit our grandparents for summer vacation. We occasionally visited our cousins in Flint, Michigan. I can remember on one occasion, we went to visit our cousins and we enjoyed ourselves all day. Later that night I was awakened by one of my older female cousins who was sexually abusing me, she was probably doing what had been done to her. I screamed to the top of my lungs and my father packed us up and we went home. I was once again labeled as the troublemaker. We've never seen our cousins since that night.

Words are powerful and labels have a way of following you. On one occasion I was babysitting my younger siblings and my boyfriend came to see me. He said he needed to talk to me in private. I was not expecting what happened next. He overpowered me then he raped me. I was not supposed to let him in the house, but I did not expect him to hurt me! I was the victim, but I was blamed for what happened to me in the end, because I let him in the house.

The hardest thing for me as a child was overhearing a conversation between my father and another woman, which would change my life forever! I told my mother what I heard, my parents argued, my father left and eventually they got a divorce after twenty-four years of marriage. This time I BLAMED MYSELF! The friction between my mother and I was too much for me and I ran away from home.

I ran right into my boyfriend's arms. We moved in with some friends that had their own home. This was unheard of in those days. We were all the same age and still in high school. I stayed there for a few months until I found out they were dealing drugs so I had to leave. Even with all I had been through I still had a **Definiteness of Purpose** to finish high school. I was determined not to live in poverty and to become self-sufficient! I graduated from Mackenzie High School in 1972!

A FRESH START, A NEW NAME AND A NEW ME

I became a part of a church called the Shrine of the Black Madonna in 1972 along with my two sisters. The Shrine taught me self-love and how to be proud of who I was! We had an African naming ceremony and a gentleman from Africa gave me the name Nefertiti. I only saw him once, but the name stuck out in my mind. Nefertiti was the Queen of the Nile River, she was also beautiful, fearless and relentless! The thought that someone was calling me a Queen after all I had been through, changed how I felt about myself!

The Shrine was helping me change my life. I had finally broken up with my boyfriend because we were going in different directions. However, I found out I was pregnant and told him about the pregnancy. He wanted to get married, but I was determined to escape the depression and poverty that I saw in Detroit. I wanted a better life for my child! He decided no one else could have us if he couldn't have us. One day I was walking to the bus stop on my way to the Shrine and he walked up behind me. He grabbed me and dragged me down the street! He took me into a friend's basement apartment and threw me in the bathtub. *He was in a drug-induced rage.* He beat me, kicked me and choked me within an inch of my life! He stopped short of killing me because he had blown his high with all of the energy he exerted. He told me he was going to get high again and when he came back *he was going to kill me!* **HE DID NOT GET A CHANCE**! He went in one direction and I ran in the other direction. I didn't know where I was going. I just kept running! The next thing I knew, his brother was putting me in a cab and sending me to my sisters. I went to the hospital and by God's grace; there was no problem with my child! I only had to wear a splint on my arm for three weeks because I had torn ligaments. God had other plans for us and my oldest son was born in 1973, and he was *full of life*!

I was working in the office at the Shrine and met someone new. We started dating and fell in love. He was the first person to introduce me to the concept of a **Positive Mental Attitude.** He would always say; "*Whatever man can conceive and believe, he can achieve*". The Shrine decided to open up a new church in Atlanta and he was transferred. I was ready to get married, but he wasn't, we broke up and this time I tried to commit suicide! My sister found me and rushed me to the hospital. God was not through with me yet! I had to learn how to love myself.

For the next couple of years I concentrated on taking care of my son and getting my life together. I did Missionary work for the church and sang in the choir. Then *HE* walked into my life! It was *LOVE AT FIRST SIGHT*! The very first time I saw Robert (Hodari Taifa), I knew I would be his wife! He walked through the doors of the Shrine's Training Center and I told my sister I was going to marry him. Robert and I got to know each other and became best friends. Ironically we tried to help each other mend our broken relationships. Once we finally realized that was futile, we took our relationship to the next level. We moved to Houston to start a new life, got married in 1979 and became a blended family. I soon suppressed all the horrible things that had happened to me and never really talked about them or dealt with them again.

LIFE WAS GOOD

We arrived in Houston with $700 to our name, but we were optimistic about making a new life for our family. I got a job at a Steel manufacturing plant the day we arrived!

I later went to work for an Industrial equipment company through a temporary agency. They hired me full time because I believed in **Teamwork** and had **Self-discipline**. I started out doing keyboard entry and my memory helped me learn ten-key by touch. I was promoted to Computer Operator and learned how to operate several IBM computers. I eventually managed the computer department.

After the birth of our youngest son in 1981 I became a stay at home mom until 1985. I worked a few temporary jobs to help Robert maintain the home. I also started singing with a group called Split Image. We sang at different venues around Houston. I even did talent shows with a company called the People's Workshop. I won a few awards, was offered a contract and asked to go on the road. I declined because my family was more Important.

In 1985 I started working for Benefits Design Group an agency for Guardian Life Insurance. Things were in total disarray and the company was only producing a few hundred thousand dollars a year. I worked part time, but after a few months I was offered a full time position and eventually replaced the New Business clerk. I took **Personal Initiative** and organized the department to increase efficiency. I was quickly promoted from New Business clerk to Underwriting Director. The General Agent Mr. Dennis Manning and I put together a model of what would be used to track business at Guardian Life Insurance, known as the New Business Tracking system. We quickly became one of the premier agencies in the Guardian Life Insurance system. Mr. Manning went on to become the President of Guardian Life Insurance in New York in 1991.

When Mr. Granville Knight became the new General Agent in 1991, he brought his own staff with him. Though I kept my salary, my title was changed to New Business Analyst and my life seemed like it was going backwards at first. However, I got sick and had to have surgery. The fact that I had less responsibilities worked in my favor because I had to be off of work for several months. Mr. Knight retired in 1999.

Mr. Gary Kinder became General Agent and my life started taking a forward turn. I became the Sr. New Business Analyst and worked under Mr. Kinder from 1999-2004.

In 2004 Mr. Rick Ray became General Agent of Wealth Design Group (WDG). I am currently the Sr. New Business Analyst for WDG. I also train new agents on the underwriting process. WDG has been voted one of the best places to work in Houston on two occasions and the company currently produces millions of dollars annually. These accomplishments were made possible through the collaborative effort of **Teamwork** through service to others. I am proud to say I played a significant role in making these accomplishments possible. WDG also made a tremendous difference for my family when Robert was sick. After his death, a plaque was hung on the wall in our main conference room in remembrance of him and my co-workers husband that also died of cancer. I now have a greater appreciation for what is needed when I receive a request for life or disability insurance, because of my own personal experience. Therefore, I try to treat each case as if it is for a member of my family. I am grateful for the owners Mr. and Mrs. Rick and Tara Ray and the culture that has been created at WDG.

MY FATHER TAUGHT ME SURVIVAL SKILLS

In 1987 my youngest son and I were returning from Detroit on Continental Airlines. There were a few problems with our plane and after several delays; they redirected all passengers flying to Houston, to board *Northwest Airlines Flight 255*. We had already been in the airport for twelve and a half hours and I was tired, frustrated, and did not want to move. I refused to get on that plane! All the other Houston bound passengers gladly transferred. Moments later, we heard a loud crashing noise. The Northwest plane crashed into a bridge right after takeoff and all of its passengers were killed except a four-year-old girl. I still didn't realize all the miracles that God had already worked in my life, I was terrified!

In 1989 my father joined Amway and we became one of his distributors. This was the first time we were introduced to Network Marketing. It didn't last long, because there was no system in place. However, a good friend of ours re-introduced us to Amway and we quickly adapted. We couldn't wait to get to the meetings because there was always a positive atmosphere! The first self-help book we were introduced to was Think and Grow Rich, by Napoleon Hill! Becoming part of Amway also helped Robert and I stop smoking. Though we enjoyed Amway, we made very little money. Robert grew tired and we decided it was no longer for us.

We were living comfortably, but I still wanted more. In 2000 I joined a company called Artistic Impressions and became an Art Broker. Robert wanted no part of it until I became a leader and he saw the amount of my checks. I was making more on some of those checks than I was at my job. He decided he would help me set up for my presentations. *Unfortunately*, this too would end soon.

OUR LIVES WERE TURNED UPSIDE DOWN

Robert's mother died in 2001, he grieved tremendously and began to smoke again. In 2003 because of an automobile accident, doctor's discovered Robert had a rare form of cancer called Multiple Myeloma. Robert was hospitalized and this was a very critical time in his life! I brought in all of our children and grandchildren, which included his daughter and grandson from North Carolina. A few of his sisters also flew in from Michigan. Our goal was to uplift his spirits and give him the will to live! We all rallied around him as a family and he decided he wanted to fight! He had to wear a Bremer Halo on his head to stabilize his neck (like the one Superman had to wear). He only had a slither of his third cervical vertebra left. His doctor planned to do surgery after he removed the Halo. Miraculously, his neck fused back together in nine months, *surgery was not necessary*! However, doctor's put him on permanent disability. Suddenly I became the breadwinner of the family as well as his caregiver. His prognosis was eleven months, but Robert lived for seven years! We pulled from every Success Principle we had ever learned to help us, and we began *The Fight of our Lives*!

We were **PROACTIVE** and became students of his disease! We both had a **Positive Mental Attitude.** Our **Definiteness of Purpose** was for Robert to live and not die and declare the works of the Lord! We researched the disease and used alternative medicine along with chemotherapy and radiation. We **Applied Faith**, changed our environment and our diets! Robert did Tai Chi on a daily basis to help him Center and Focus his mind on **Maintaining Sound Health**! We used healing scriptures daily and prayed the Prayer of Jabeez. Whenever Robert had to travel, he could not just sit down in the car because of the Halo. I would grab one hand and brace myself against the car with the other hand. He would squat down and lean backwards into the car. Once his body made it in I would put his legs in. We had to repeat it in reverse when he got out of the car. Robert was 5'8" and weighed 238 lbs., I was 5'7" and 160 lbs. One time I was pushing him across the street in a wheelchair, we were not far from the curb, but the light changed and cars were coming at a high speed. I had to pick the wheelchair up with him in it or risk the chance of us both getting hit! It is amazing how God gives you strength when you really need it!

The medical bills kept piling up so I decided to get a second job. I worked two jobs for a year and we were beginning to see light at the end of the tunnel.

ANOTHER ACCIDENT CHANGED OUR LIVES AGAIN

Robert had begun to feel better and the cancer was in remission. He was now able to drive. One day we were in route to my second job, I was driving. Robert was riding with me so he could pick me up after work because it would be dark. My second job was only ten minutes away from our home. Not only did we do this for my safety, sometimes that was all the time we had to spend together. *WE NEVER MADE IT!* We were in an accident and we were both injured. I ended up being off of work for seven months. I also developed claustrophobia. I never returned to the part time job but I pushed myself to go back to work at my full time job. We had to have an income because of Robert's medical needs.

Hurricane Ike struck Houston right in the middle of *OUR STORM!* We could not travel because of Robert's disability, so we rode the storm out. Tornadoes spun around our area and damaged our roof! We had to leave our home and move in with our son and daughter-in-law. We could not live in our home for months. We had to be transported everywhere until the doctor released me to go back to work. Our faith was truly being tested!

TRIALS KEEP YOU STRONG

Robert's cancer returned and this time he succumbed the day

before my fifty-sixth birthday in 2010. I didn't realize I lost myself while I was taking care of him. Since his death, I've had to re-live and reconstruct my entire life. I had to find out who I was before him, while I was with him and now who I am supposed to become. Grief was complicated for me because all of the hurt I suppressed for more than thirty years resurfaced and I had to deal with it as well. I had to learn to open up and allow myself to be vulnerable and allow others to help me. I had to learn to love myself and also forgive those I had shut out of my life because I felt they hurt me, or didn't protect me, when I thought they should have. Even though I forgave, I still had not let go of the brokenness that continued to be a part of my life.

My three remaining grandparents died within six months of Robert being diagnosed with cancer. I was able to attend my paternal grandmother's funeral. Unfortunately I missed the funerals of both of my maternal grandparents.

After Robert's death, I lost my home to foreclosure. I lost my car and all kinds of stuff in my storage facility. I was living in a two-bedroom apartment and decided I was ready to move. The search became a lot more difficult than I anticipated when I discovered there were some problems with my credit that I was not aware of. I had to move in with my son and daughter-in-law, for the second time. Even though it was what I needed, it was the hardest thing for me to do, because it humbled me! My sons became my teachers and reminded me of the things I taught them. For instance, make every experience a learning experience and never let go of your dreams! The hard truth was that I was just existing. I walked around as if I was okay, but I was in denial. I was being eaten alive!

GIVE AND IT SHALL BE GIVEN UNTO YOU

They say the more people you help get what they want the more you will get what you want.

To Whom Much Is Given Much Is Required

Since my husband's death there have been several individuals that have pushed me towards my purpose. I have always had the ability to encourage others to do things they did not believe they could. I asked God for *Greatness*, but it wasn't until I started being *Grateful* those things started to change! When I took my eyes off of myself and stopped having a pity party, things start falling into place! While some people would consider these things as **Going the Extra Mile**, I did what comes natural to me.

Though I was still going through my own storm my oldest sister became very ill and had to be hospitalized for more than a month. I had to become her *encourager* and help her push past her limitations!

One of my closest friends was suddenly fighting a battle with her health. I was there to help her push through it. She now uses Organo (the Healthier Lifestyle Company), coffees, teas, meal replacement shakes and nutraceuticals and is sharing them with others because of the positive effect they have had in her life!

Another friend was hospitalized in ICU, visits were restricted because of that. One day I was headed home, but went to the hospital instead, determined to see her. I know GOD is still in the miracle working business! When I got there she did not look like herself and didn't recognize me. We talked and prayed for a few hours until she called me by my nickname. I knew it was God! I started calling everybody I could think of to cheer her up. They were all elated to hear her voice. She was more elated to hear their voices and seemed determined to keep fighting.

Tai Chi helped prolong Roberts life! Now I attend a Tai Chi class weekly. Ironically the instructor, Henderson Smith, is my former co-worker. I helped him when he was just getting started with the company we worked for, now he is helping me!

WHY? – SEASONED WOMEN OF PURPOSE (S.W.O.P.)

In June 2011, I was watching the last episodes of the Oprah Winfrey show and Tyler Perry was introducing the more than three hundred African American Males Oprah helped get a scholarship to Morehouse College. I was on my bed crying myself to sleep as usual and sat straight up and asked God to send me a vehicle that would allow me to be used for *greatness*!

A few days later the phone rang and a friend extended an invitation for me to come take a look at something. I almost missed the opportunity because we were not really on the best of terms. I told him I would think about it and call him back. He told me he needed a commitment because of the caliber of the person that would be sharing an opportunity with us. When I hung up the phone I heard a voice saying…you asked me to send you a vehicle and your pride is going to make you miss it. *I CALLED HIM BACK THE NEXT DAY*! Before the presentation was over I knew I wanted to be a part of it because it was what I prayed for! I became an Independent Distributor for the Healthier Lifestyle company in 2011 and it has changed my life! The person doing the presentation is now my Coach Mr. Edwin Haynes.

The Healthier Lifestyle Company has products that add a health component to people's habit. I believe we have the best products, the best company and the best leadership! We have been allowed to participate in a business that is normally only available to the rich and for that I am truly grateful! I am a product of the product and believe I have found the fountain of youth! We often say the Healthier Lifestyle Company is a personal self-development company with a compensation plan attached to it. I truly believe that the things I've learned in this company has made a difference in every aspect of my life! I am so happy and grateful for the association with the leadership of the company. Thank you to our CEO Mr. and Mrs. Bernardo and Adeline Chua, Global Master Distributor Mr. and Mrs. Shane and Josie Morand, CVO Mr. and Mrs. Holton and Earlene Buggs. Thank you to my direct line of leadership of Mr. and Mrs. Edwin and Andrea Haynes and Ms. Nyya Linscomb. To Mr. and Mrs. Eddie and Rita Stallworth thank you for introducing me to this business!

I am currently a part of a **Mastermind Alliance** of women that helps each other through difficult times. We help each other set goals and then keep each other accountable to those goals! My finances, my spiritual life, my family bond, my health and my career have tremendously improved! Thank you to my

Goal Getting Sisters!

They say in life you don't get what you want you get what you picture. I have a Vision Board on my wall with the words *Best Selling Author* in the center. My vision is coming to life as I collaborate in the writing of this book. For six years I have posted a certain dollar amount on my walls. I recently received a raise for that *EXACT* amount!

Today I live in an intimate one bedroom, one bath condo. I didn't think I would be able to handle it because of my claustrophobia. God has a sense of humor! I am the happiest and most grateful that I have been for most of my life! I understand that if I am grateful in the small things he would give me the desires of my heart.

My late husband was my soul mate; I spent almost half my life with him. He will forever be a part of my life and I must finish what we started. We always wanted to make a difference in the lives of others. My goal is to help others obtain Economic Power!

I continue to push forward to be an example for my family and to leave them a legacy!

To my son Akiiki, daughter-law Melody, son Hodari, stepdaughter, Tishauna, son-in-law, Jay, grandchildren Christopher, Johnathan, Akila, Jayden, JayVaughn and Jaymarri and my great grandson, Ayden... I love you all from the depths of my soul!

Now I understand, my mother taught me how to have determination, perseverance and a strong faith. My father taught me how to work for myself and that I deserved the finer things in life! I love my family from the bottom of my heart! At the end of 2016, I cruised to the Bahamas with my mother and most of my siblings, it was wonderful! We parasailed, snorkeled and went horseback riding on the beach.

DEFINITENESS OF PURPOSE :

- My God given purpose is that of encouragement. My vision is to encourage, inspire, impact and empower others to believe in themselves and make a difference in other people's lives!
- My goal is to become a person of significance and help others break generational curses. I will do this by helping them develop a **Positive Mental Attitude**. Thereby changing their family's legacy.
- I plan to travel the world to share my story, to show others, God uses imperfect people for his glory.
- I have a vision to help 100 families earn a 7-figure income and change the financial fabric of *our* lives, while we enrich the lives of thousands around the world.
- I also have a goal to donate $100,000/ea to the Multiple Myeloma Foundation and International Myeloma Foundation in my late husband's name, Robert H. Patton.

It was not easy to open up and allow others into my private life. I realize that the things I went through were not for me, they were to benefit others. Being transparent is allowing me to LET GO so that I don't continue to live the hurt! It is my hope that my story will inspire someone else to believe they were born for greatness, no matter what they have been through! I am the sum total of everyone that has made a contribution to my life. I am eternally grateful for ALL the life lessons I have learned, even those that were painful!

To Whom Much Is Given Much Is Required

I gave my husband a greeting card called the *"The Oak Tree"* I now realize that card was for me!

"The Oak Tree"

A mighty wind blew night and day,
It stole the oak tree's leaves away
Then snapped its boughs and pulled its bark
Until the oak was tired and stark
But still the oak tree held its ground
While other trees fell all around
The weary wind gave up and spoke,
"How can you still be standing, Oak?"

...

Until today I wasn't sure
Of just how much I could endure
But now I've found, with thanks to you
I'm stronger than I ever knew!

"VICTORY IS ALWAYS POSSIBLE FOR THE PERSON WHO REFUSES TO STOP FIGHTING!"

— Napoleon Hill

BIO | Linda (Nefertiti) Patton

Linda lives in Houston, Texas and works as the Sr. New Business Analyst for the Financial Planning Firm, Wealth Design Group. She has worked in this industry for 32 years and works diligently to fulfill the needs of their clients.

    As an Independent distributor her goal is to help individuals obtain a healthier alternative to what they habitually do on a daily basis. Linda knows the products that she markets through the Healthier Lifestyle Company would have been a healthier alternative for her husband that she lost to cancer in 2010. Though Linda has received recognition for reaching several different levels with the Healthier Lifestyle Company, she is just getting started. She envisions making a difference in the lives of thousands worldwide.

    Linda is a widow and has 2 sons, a stepdaughter, 6 grandchildren and 1 great grandson. Linda participated in a Let Go Let God boot camp with Regina Baker and the testimonials of the ladies started the wheels to rolling in her life. She is now

To Whom Much Is Given Much Is Required

sharing the adversities she has overcome in hopes of helping others as well. Linda enjoys singing, dancing, making others laugh and has several other hobbies. She uses Tai Chi and Yoga to stay fit.

For more information you may reach Linda at

713-679-3837 or send an email to lpatton11@hotmail.com

Please visit the following websites for more information:

The Healthier Lifestyle Company
www.rhpatton.organogold.com

Wealth Design Group - www.wealthdesigngroup.net

CHAPTER 14

Samson vs Goliath: Using PMA To Grow A Startup Against Cable Giants

By: Mark English

My life has been a journey with a solid foundation of understanding change, different cultures and relocation. I am someone who has a firm belief in the need to push your own limits in order to find out who we are.

Moving away from Canada as a child, I spent a good chunk of my youth growing up in Connecticut. During this time, I attended 6 different schools and lived in 11 different places. We moved around quite a bit and it was tough for my parents to see me having to make new friends every year or two at each place we went. Change was something that quickly became the norm for me. The adversity of changing school boards, classes and friends was something that I truly believe is what made me who I am as an adult.

People always say that they want to provide a better life for their children. This usually translates into parents allowing more freedoms for their kids. My parents certainly tried to give me an easier life than they had growing up. Luckily for me, it wasn't easy. I think that when given the opportunity to be "comfortable", most people will jump at the chance, which is what in my opinion is the worst thing that you can do for someone. The struggle, the drive to succeed and the inevitable roller coaster ride that is life is what, to me, brings the thrill and unknown into daily situations.

I bring all of this up to of course bring it back to my life experience. Fast-forward until I'm finished school and have set out into the world to become the best that I can be. Unfortunately, school doesn't prepare you for the realities of being an adult. I started to go through what a lot of young people struggle with, a lack of direction. Even without technology being what it is now, one thing has stayed the same for a very long time that most people don't have a plan for their lives and the ones who do, usually don't follow it the way they intended.

My main problem as a new adult was not the worry of what I would do and what I would become but rather how long I could take advantage of how comfortable I had become as a young man who spent a few years at this point, firmly planted in one spot. This was not normal for me but it sure felt nice.

A few years went by feeling this way and enjoying my comforts until around the age of 22 when my father's willingness to let me continue drifting started to wear thin. I knew I needed to start planning my future, even though for years I have experienced almost zero motivation pursuing a preferred career path. I'll mention as well that I had had several health issues relating to back and gastrointestinal problems. These things made justifying my lifestyle even easier.

I spoke to a friend that I hadn't talked to very often since high school who was living and teaching English in China. The idea of doing that terrified me but also intrigued me.

I started to try to put it in my head in a place imagining that I would go and join him to do something for myself to establish independence and learn to work hard. It took almost a year to finally convince myself that it was something that I had to do to remove the comfort factor from my life.

At this point, I had to convince my girlfriend who lived with me and who had been in a relationship with me since we were 16, that this is something I needed as well as that she should find her own motivation too. Leaving a person who I loved and leave a comfortable situation to move across the planet to a place I've never been before and didn't speak the language was,,,,, tough.

I quickly adapted, as I knew how to do from my youth, and a six-week exploratory trip turned into more than five years and three cities of experiencing everything that was completely different than anything before. My girlfriend that I split from to travel; met up with me during her travels and we quickly became very involved again, but with a new perspective. We eventually married after returning home to the place we were most familiar with, Canada.

Everything I've spoken about, while it has its own unique situations, is not that much different than the internal struggles that most young people must overcome to become what they want to be. Returning to Canada was a completely backwards situation than what I thought. We both viewed China as a part of our lives that we got our act together and worked hard in a place that requires a certain type of outlook to succeed. We thought Canada would be easier and we would be even happier, which didn't turn out to be this way. Quickly I became caught up in the endless cycle of trying to be "normal". The thing I noticed most about people here is that small problems seemed bigger than they were. I learned the term "*first world problems*" which is just term to used in branding problems that shouldn't be problems. These "*problems*" are in my opinion what is creating an environment where negativity breeds. I started to catch myself doing this. I don't know how long I had been doing it, or how bad it had become. I just knew that it was something that getting worse and my happiness was diminishing, even though I had more in life than ever before.

The phone rang late night almost a year ago from writing this. My father was in the hospital having suffered a heart attack. There was no bigger moment for me to start thinking about life, a little bit more. He recovered and is healthy as ever but I realized that now I need to think about my future. I set out to be better, healthier and happier. The problem with this is that I had no idea how to make this change, whom to talk to, or even how to begin obtaining this life change for myself. The first article I read from searching the internet about how to become a better person, told me that happiness is all internal. This immediately resonated with me from seeing people on the street corners in Shanghai of poor neighborhoods playing card games. They are playing games on a makeshift table and chairs where every night it seems they are having the best evening they can. AIt was always the same guys, doing the same thing, enjoying themselves. Thinking about this, I instantly realized that the internet article was right. I immediately stopped reading further articles and set out to figure out how to be more like the guys in Shanghai who have very little.

    I spent months attempting to do the things that I thought would help me in my journey. Things like biting my tongue when I normally would react, saying nice things to others, helping strangers as well as once and awhile eating something healthier. I started to realize that it wasn't those things that were making me happier; it was the thought process of associating those things with happiness and then doing them. Once I realized that just trying to think more positively actually made me more positive, the benefits started becoming evident. My work life, friendships, family and most importantly, my wife started to seem happier around me. I am certainly not trying to say that it has made an impact in their lives, although I hope it did. I can only assume that I was just becoming someone that they wanted to be around more than before. I'm now using my newfound "*happiness*" and applying it to all those things including working harder. I've started to practice Mandarin again, which I learned years ago in. I fear Change less, talk more, and when I'm feeling stressed, I have more to remind me that most things that are tough in my life are just part of life. Some things I can change, some things I can't, which is very different than my previous way of thinking, which was to try and change everything that I didn't see as "*ideal*".

An Entrepreneur and a Manufacturer

MyGica in North America started in 2011 when an entrepreneur recognized a technology and opportunity that will one day become the norm for television watchers. At that time, Netflix was a new company, and almost nobody had any idea that there would be a new way for them to take control of their TV watching and paying coming soon.

We decided at MyGica, that we wanted the best product on the market and to do that we would need to partner with an exceptional manufacturer. After a lot of research and due diligence we chose to partner with Geniatech and we are very happy that we did. Their professionalism as a company, and their commitment to be the best engineered and manufactured android box company in the world, has helped us to grow MyGica faster than even we predicted.

Geniatech's commitment to our partnership is so solid that we have never lost sleep over some of the typical issues that plague a new partnership. Geniatech's management has such a high level of integrity that they have always consulted us about potential hardware limitations on the horizon. They have also been the first to always share with us what they think could be a feature on a potential new product, based on their technological research and development teams. In the past, competitors have tried to partner with our manufacturer, to which they are always referred directly back to us for business.

Geniatech is based in China; and as a Mandarin speaker, I am one of the main contacts to speak with each division of Geniatech. It helps break the ice quickly whenever a new person at Geniatech joins in on overseeing all things MyGica. Because I enjoyed the time I spent teaching English in China several years before I joined MyGica, I like going back to experience their culture and food and new technologies whenever I get the chance.

Changing the Television Watching Experience

According to Wikipedia, cable television started in 1948 in the United States and in 1952 in Canada. Today, in 2017, 65 to 70 years later, most people are still paying a monthly cable bill. Not only do most people pay for a cable package, they also rent PVR recorders and boxes from their cable companies. They also pay tax on top of those fees.

In an article in September 2016, Fortune magazine said that the average cable bill is $103 per month. In Canada, CBC reported that, in 2015, the average cable bill was $66, not including the monthly rental of PVR boxes and, as always, taxes.

For a good percentage of today's Millennials, they have never paid a monthly cable bill and they watch most of their content on tablets and phones. But even they spend a fair amount of time watching television.

MyGica's ATSC android boxes allow you to either eliminate your monthly cable bill, or lower it substantially and still get the majority of your local television channels as well as lots of on demand television and movie content.

Many people who are using Netflix, Amazon Prime or any other streaming platform for much or most of watching time until recently, have been watching it on their tablets and phones but not their televisions unless they buy the overpriced "Smart" TV's that are everywhere. MyGica enables you to watch a variety of these apps on your television and, because it is on the android platform, you have access to millions of apps including lots that you can watch almost every show and movie you can think of.

In the United States, apps like Crackle, Hulu, Amazon Prime Video, HBO Go and Sling will give you enough on-demand, commercial free content to keep you happy and content the rest of your television watching years.

Another technology that has brought on this revolution in how people are choosing to watch and pay for their local tv channels are ATSC tuners, known as an Over-the-Air Antenna.

Picture the antennas people used in the early days of cable, rabbit ears as they were often referred to. Today's ATSC antenna is small, compact and very low cost. They allow you to get your local channels, public broadcasting stations and other channels for free in HD.

By using both an Over-the-Air Antenna and a MyGica box, you will have access to more content than your cable company can typically offer you, and at a much lower monthly cost.

Turn Every TV into a Smart TV

My father recently called me, all excited because he had purchased a $1600 55 inch 4k Smart TV, paying over $500 more for a larger 65 inch non-smart 4k TV of the same brand. Using the same positive attitude that I always used on the support line with our customers, I suggested he return the TV, purchase a larger, non-smart one for a lot less money and turn that larger TV into a smart one for less than $200. He followed my advice and was happy to have saved all that money and be able to purchase one with a larger screen.

Why would you pay $500 or more for a smart TV when you could purchase a larger screen and get the smart part for less than $200?

One of the best things about our android boxes is that you can literally plug it in and have it working in less than 5 minutes by simply plugging in a couple of cables before you can explore the world of app based media.

Using PMA to Convert Anger to Happiness

Most people would find this odd but I love turning an upset and frustrated customer into a happy and educated one. Not many people enjoy conversations where the other person is upset and angry right from the start. I don't "*enjoy*" those conversations either, however, I do enjoy using my PMA to not only make sure they get their questions get answered and resolved but also to help them get the most out of their android box, by explaining its many uses and applications. For me, I believe most people want to be happier using their latest technology but often get stuck on the things that make them lose their patience.

With over a million MyGica customers at the moment, one of my main jobs is to teach and educate customers and potential consumers about their viewing options and help make the switch from cable as painless and seamless as possible, even if our products aren't quite right for them at the time.

An Easy Way To Save Over $1000 In The Next 12 Months

Most people in North America have some money challenges and would really like to save over $1000 a year that they would have already been spending. You can save that $1000 annually, and often much more, by purchasing a MyGica android box and an Over-the-Air Antenna, for a total of less than $200 and subscribing to apps like Crackle, Hulu, Amazon Prime and others for your on demand shows and movies.

BIO | Mark English

Mark English is a young man who's travelled the world in the pursuit of fulfillment and happiness through increased motivation, positivity and perspective.

Mark has had both great success and failure in his time on this planet. Through life's ups and downs, he has chosen to be happier than ever before, utilizing outside sources from online as well as his own techniques. Recognizing that not every person is the same, he has found that everything starts with a combination of baby steps, as well as large strides when presented with the opportunity.

Spend a short time with Mark as he talks about the keys to his own personal success. His journey has similarities to most young people finding their way, as well as a few things he chose to do that were very against the grain of what is considered the "norm".

As a young child, Mark was, as he proclaims, "given the opportunity" to overcome typical self confidence issues that all people do growing up through the process of having to move so often. It's the adversity as a young boy that he feels so strongly about what made him into the person he is today.

Mark spends great amounts of time trying to help others in his job, with his friends and most importantly, any stranger who is willing to accept a friendly gesture. He enjoys sharing stories of times being called out for a poor judgment as well as when he has changed a bad day into a good one. A lot of the stories are not giant acts of kindness and a lot of time are simply telling about how much a smile and a thank you will go to brighten up someone's day who may have just held the door open for you, or simply let you go first in line at the store.

CHAPTER 15

What Will You Do To Change?

By: Antony Scandale

Essence of Prosperity

The title *"Essence of Prosperity"* is an ever-changing concept. How you feel about prosperity today may change at any given moment.

It is to suggest, what is most valuable to you, right now?

Shelter, sustenance, and clothing are all invaluable commodities to maintain life. Moreover, having a steady job to help fund those aforementioned necessities coupled with a little extra money for entertainment, to many, is worth more than a king's ransom.

I had all of that and perhaps more than some, and yet deep within my consciousness I was missing a few key elements of living a full and happy life.

This is not to devalue precious metals, mansions, and other lavish things most long for. Many authors within this book have achieved success beyond their imagination and deservedly so.

A simple parable comes to mind.

The Naked Man

A man is tired, naked and without shelter. He is dehydrated and hasn't eaten for days. His arms and legs have become so weakened by the lack of nourishment, that he can barely lift his arms off of the ground.

Although his death is imminent, he continues to crawl forward without any destination in mind. Movement is his only hope for survival. Moment's later a woman in fine clothing greets him as he lies on his stomach, dying.

> *"You have two choices, to my right is a table filled with food and water, enough to restore your strength and provide you perfect health. Thus, you will be given a second chance at life. On my left, is a 1000-pound sack of gold coins, enough to buy you a luxurious mansion, the finest garments, and you shall be sated for the rest of your life. However, you must walk away with this sack on your shoulders and without any help. What do you choose?"*

He ponders for a moment, but his ability to make a rational decision wanes. He does but say through his chapped and withered lips, *"Please, help me up. A second chance at life is more valuable than gold."*

That Was Then

In a lot of ways, I was the complete opposite of the man in the parable. In my haste, my boorish bravado would have chosen the gold coins.

My life was marred with jealousy, hatred, and fear – a recipe for: self-loathing, low self-worth, and depression.

I didn't see the true value of life. I expected everything to be gifted to me. Even though I wasn't the desperate and destitute man in the parable my life felt poor because of my worthless and sour attitude.

Many new opportunities were missed because of my clouded vision. I could not see past the fog of negativity. No matter the lesson behind every consequential experience, I shunned at the opportunity to learn from it and to understand the underlying message.

I would cast the blame of my problems on everyone else instead of taking full responsibility for my actions. I pushed away any inkling of purpose, which sat, dormant within me.

I reached my darkest moment after three life changing events took place. I was working overnight shifts at a dead end job I hated, my girlfriend broke up with me, and to make matters worse, my grandmother died two weeks later.

I was broken and I had no one to turn to. I didn't have a mentor or a support group. I was alone with my feelings of despair and anguish and I did not know how to release the past.

I was taught not to cry or show my emotions. *"Real men don't cry!"* I believed. And yet I was still willing to talk to someone, but I had no one who wanted to hear my story.

I was rapidly heading toward the side of life I had often dreaded as a child. Even though the destination to destitution wasn't on the horizon, in my mind I was convinced I had a one-way ticket to *"Nowheresville"*.

After my grandmother's funeral, I quit my job and move back home. Life happened and I didn't know how to deal with it.

I was broke, jobless, alone and unhappy and it was at this point I realized I needed to find a better way.

"There had to be a better way."

The Desire for Transformation

In his book, *Think and Grow Rich*, Napoleon Hill describes the importance of the first step toward change, which is 'having a burning desire for achievement'.

The thought of 'taking-a-leap-of-faith-into-the-unknown' was frightening and gave me butterflies in my stomach. And yet, that sensation, gave me a sense of clarity and excitement. I kept hearing an inner voice saying, *"Make your decision to change and stick with it."*

Days after my decision, I met a gentleman who spoke about personal growth and development. When we met, it was clear to him that I needed to focus on what he calls *"deprogramming the mind."* He told me that I had to change in all areas of my life and he had the tools and techniques to help me through it. Moreover, he assured me that I had the innate ability to live a happier and healthier life.

I never questioned his teachings; my heart knew that I had to follow along with his instruction. When it was time to cry, I cried. When it was time to meditate, I meditated, when it was time to forgive, I forgave.

I never gave up. I worked through it all no matter how hard the process got.

If I had unkind thoughts or if I was triggered to feel aggressive or sad I was told to stop, and then pause to breathe and change my thinking.

He made it clear 'that life begins with a thought first and once the thought is attached to an emotion it can be made manifest into physical reality.'

This was my problem. Anything and everything, which had happened to me, was because of my sour thinking. Hence, it brought forth negativity in the form of negative people and a negative bank account.

The Breakthrough

One day, after doing some heavy, release work on family members, I started to cry. An overwhelming sense of relief and happiness took over me.

I was no longer mad or angry with my loved ones. In its place came a wave of pure love and respect for each individual.

It was the breakthrough I had been waiting for and I am convinced that forgiveness is the key to unlocking the inner power within your heart!

The key is to let go of what no longer serves you and to allow for your heart to begin the healing process!

For months, I continued on with my meditation sessions and more wonderful changes began to happen. My body started to crave healthy food and my mind wanted to read self-help books and only think and speak positively. As for my soul, it wanted to travel the world and learn to love again.

Some of the most valuable lessons I learned from him were – 'always be grateful, love thyself and others, always let go, move forward and find the positive within everything'.

This Is Now

To say that I am 100% better would be a lie. Self-improvement is an ongoing journey. There is always room for growth however, I have never felt this good in my life!

After years of deprogramming and reprogramming, my life is much more fluid and feels light and in sync with the universe. I have made amends with the past and I approach life with ease and confidence.

I have learned that life is simply about expanding the mind and finding new ways to feel better and better. You can always better your best.

I still cry, I still meditate, and I still forgive, when necessary, but I always give thanks for what I have and for what is coming.

My gratitude list goes beyond the tangibles. I am grateful that I can teach to those who need to hear my message. I am grateful I can get up in the morning under my own strength. I am grateful to be alive and to serve my purpose. I am grateful to have stayed committed to my commitment. Above all, I am grateful to have experienced my darkest moments.

If I hadn't had that 'burning desire to change' I would have remained stagnant. However, with a lot of hard work I was able to release my past. This freed me to travel the world, spend 10 months in Florence, Italy learning Italian, and to go on to write my first book entitled Let Go: A Little Guidebook to Freedom; an accomplishment I am proud of, which could never have been written without going through my experiences.

New Beginnings

Currently my *"Essence of Prosperity"* is my life's purpose, which is 'to show others that there is always a better way' and to 'always be grateful for new beginnings'.

There is great value within new beginnings and it is more valuable than all the gold in the world, but first we must learn to let go.

My friends, the process of 'letting go' is difficult and yet necessary to be able to bring in what is waiting for you. But you need to ask yourself, *"What am I willing to give up and throw out for the new?"*

When the pain, worry, and fear finally melt away the EUREKA moment is euphoric. Truth outshines the shadow of fear and creates clarity.

It is at this point when the perspective from the past changes to an undeniable, new interpretation. It provides a sense of growth, it offers a deep understanding of personal development, and gives way to the comfortable feeling of relief.

It's Your Life and Your Story

The fabric of your life when stitched with the thread of desire, purpose, and a willingness to change, can never weigh down your inner being. It shall forever cloth you, feed you, and allow you to impact others in a profound way.

It is your life and your story - remember to choose a loving and supportive group of people, who you can trust and who will help you on your journey to success. No matter how many pages are left in your book of life, there is still time to play the hero.

Be the hero.

My Gift to You

Before I close, I will leave with an exercise to help get you out of a funk. I have used this method for many years, and the results have been phenomenal.

When things are not going your way, or when you feel it is necessary to blow-off-some-steam, try going through this exercise and see how it changes your perspective.

It is important to approach this exercise with: intention, commitment, and a willingness to change.

Understand that this process may have to be repeated until you have understood the lesson(s) and until you feel better.

Learn and Burn Exercise

I have a journal at home, and on the first page, I wrote the following quote, which acts a reminder to never allow my memories and emotions to cloud my vision and weigh me down.

"What lies upon these lines, are only fragments of memories and emotions. None of this is in the 'Now' but simply in the past - where it belongs."

Find a quiet place, and then take out a piece of paper and write out the aforementioned quote on top of the page. Once you've done so, read it out loud several times and then proceed to write.

Write down anything from your past, 'whether real or imagined', which may have caused you pain and suffering.

This is your opportunity to let go of your past fears and emotions. **Remember, what you write is in the past, where it belongs.**

Whatever has happened is immediately filed away in the history books. You are NOW. You are this moment and every moment of your day you can consciously decide how to feel.

Once you have finished, go back to the top of the page, and read the quote out loud.

What Will You Do To Change?

Finally, safely, burn the paper. Once you have burned the paper say aloud the following:

> *"I forgive those and myself, whether real or imagined, and I am open to learn the lessons behind every experience I encounter."*

Next, imagine what you would like to see happen in your life. Keep it positive, light, funny, happy. Once you have the vision, take out another piece of paper and write it all down.

Provide as much detail as possible. Is it a happy and healthy life you want? Does the rest of your life involve having a loving relationship? What will your friends, family, and peers remember you for? That is up to you.

Keep this paper handy, and refer to it every so often to keep your spirits up. Your desires are possible, but only if you believe.

I invite you to ignite your inner power and watch your world change.

Change is only the beginning.

Sincerely,

Antony S. Scandale

Author of *Let Go: A Little Guidebook to Freedom*

BIO | Antony S. Scandale

Antony S. Scandale is a Canadian born writer and personal coach who lives in Victoria, British Columbia Canada. In 2002, he earned his Television Broadcasting diploma at BCIT and graduated with honours. He then went on to work at various television broadcasting stations in Vancouver and Victoria working as a technical director for live news.

In 2010, Antony left the television broadcasting industry to teach hockey and skating skills to young children at a community recreation centre in Victoria. He began using certain motivational and teaching techniques to help bring out the best performance from every student.

Antony is now on a mission to help change the lives of other people by providing guidance and clarity through coaching and writing. His mission, is to help others understand that there is 'always a better way to live life.'

What Will You Do To Change?

In 2015, he wrote and published his first book, *Let Go: A Little Guidebook to Freedom* and continues to inspire everyone he comes in contact with.

www.antonyscandale.com

www.letgobook.net

Napoleon Hill Bio

NAPOLEON HILL
(1883-1970)

"Whatever your mind can conceive and believe it can achieve."

— Napoleon Hill

American born Napoleon Hill is considered to have influenced more people into success than any other person in history. He has been perhaps the most influential man in the area of personal success technique development, primarily through his classic book Think and Grow Rich which has helped million of the people and has been important in the life of many successful people such as W. Clement Stone and Og Mandino.

Napoleon Hill was born into poverty in 1883 in a one-room cabin on the Pound River in Wise County, Virginia. At the age of 10 his mother died, and two years later his father remarried. He became a very rebellious boy, but grew up to be an incredible man. He began his writing career at age 13 as a "mountain reporter" for small town newspapers and went on to become

America's most beloved motivational author. Fighting against all class of great disadvantages and pressures, he dedicated more than 25 years of his life to define the reasons by which so many people fail to achieve true financial success and happiness in their life.

During this time he achieved great success as an attorney and journalist. His early career as a reporter helped finance his way through law school. He was given an assignment to write a series of success stories of famous men, and his big break came when he was asked to interview steel-magnate Andrew Carnegie. Mr. Carnegie commissioned Hill to interview over 500 millionaires to find a success formula that could be used by the average person. These included Thomas Edison, Alexander Graham Bell, Henry Ford, Elmer Gates, Charles M. Schwab, Theodore Roosevelt, William Wrigley Jr, John Wanamaker, William Jennings Bryan, George Eastman, Woodrow Wilson, William H. Taft, John D. Rockefeller, F. W. Woolworth, Jennings Randolph, among others.

He became an advisor to Andrew Carnegie, and with Carnegie's help he formulated a philosophy of success, drawing on the thoughts and experience of a multitude of rags-to-riches tycoons. It took Hill over 20 years to produce his book, a classic in the Personal Development field called Think and Grow Rich. This book has sold over 7 million copies and has helped thousands achieve success. The secret to success is very simple but you'll have to read the book to find out what it is!

Napoleon Hill passed away in November 1970 after a long and successful career writing, teaching, and lecturing about the principles of success. His work stands as a monument to individual achievement and is the cornerstone of modern motivation. His book, Think and Grow Rich, is the all-time best seller in the field.

The Seventeen Principles

1. **Definiteness of Purpose**
2. **Mastermind Alliance**
3. **Applied Faith**
4. **Going the Extra Mile**
5. **Pleasing Personality**
6. **Personal Initiative**
7. **Positive Mental Attitude**
8. **Enthusiasm**
9. **Self-Discipline**
10. **Accurate Thinking**
11. **Controlled Attention**
12. **Teamwork**
13. **Learning from Adversity & Defeat**
14. **Creative Vision**
15. **Maintenance of Sound Health**
16. **Budgeting Time and Money**
17. **Cosmic Habitforce**

About Tom "too tall" Cunningham

Tom "too tall" Cunningham's God-given life purpose is to encourage and inspire people to live positively with and through life's obstacles and adversities.

He does that as a Napoleon Hill Foundation Certified Instructor, Founder of Journey To Success Radio, and creator of the Amazon International #1 Bestselling series of books, Journeys To Success.

Tom has lived with Juvenile Rheumatoid Arthritis from his jaw to his toes since the age of 5, 48 years now.

During that time, he has had 4 hips, 4 knees, and 2 shoulders replaced and been hospitalized about 40 times.

Despite his physical challenges, Tom always answers AMAZING when asked how he is doing. He tells people that 80% of the time it is true and the other 20% of the time it is to remind himself that it is true.

About Brad Szollose

Brad Szollose

(pronounced zol-us)

> *"...No one knows Millennials or cross-generational management better than Brad, and it shows; our attendees are still talking about his work."*
>
> — Robbins Research International, Inc., a Tony Robbins Company

TEDx Speaker, award-winning business author and Web Pioneer Brad Szollose helps businesses and organizations dominate their industry by tapping into the treasure of a cross-generational workforce. Brad has been called The Millennial Whisperer, and his Liquid Leadership workshops show attendees how to ignite the power of their workforce and their customer base.

Brad is also a global business adviser and the foremost expert on Generational Issues and Workforce Engagement. His bestselling book, *Liquid Leadership: From Woodstock to Wikipedia*, shares Brad's journey beginning as a bootstrapped business idea in a coffee shop to C-level executive of a publicly traded company worth $26 million in just 24 short months; becoming the FIRST Internet Agency to go public in an IPO!

As a C-Suite Executive Brad applied his unique management style to a young, tech-savvy Generation X & Y Workforce producing great results; The company experienced 425% hyper-growth for 5 straight years with only 6% turnover. Brad's management model won K2 the Arthur Andersen NY Enterprise Award for Best Practices in Fostering Innovation Among Employees.

Today the world's leading business publications seek out Brad's insights on Millennials, and he has been featured in Forbes, The Huffington Post, New York Magazine, Inc., Advertising Age, The International Business Times, The Hindu Business Line and Le Journal du Dimanche to name a few, along with television, radio and podcast appearances on CBS and other media outlets.

Today Brad's programs have transformed a new generation of business leaders, helping them maximize their corporate culture, expectations, productivity, and sales growth in The Information Age.

www.ingramcontent.com/pod-product-compliance
Lightning Source LLC
LaVergne TN
LVHW051517070426
835507LV00023B/3156